he best of boyzone

Wise Publications
London / New York / Sydney / Paris / Copenhagen / Madrid

Exclusive Distributors:
Music Sales Limited
8/9 Frith Street,
London W1V 5TZ, England.

Music Sales Pty Limited
120 Rothschild Avenue
Rosebery, NSW 2018, Australia.

Order No. AM954019
ISBN 0-7119-7209-5

Visit the Internet Music Shop at http://www.musicsales.co.uk

Music arranged by Derek Jones.
Music processed by Paul Ewers Music Design.
Book design by Michael Bell Design.
Photographs courtesy of
All Action & London Features International.

Printed in the United Kingdom by
Caligraving Limited, Thetford, Norfolk.

FILA
COWBOYS

A's

said and done

a different beat

where we belong

arms of mary

Words & Music by Iain Sutherland.

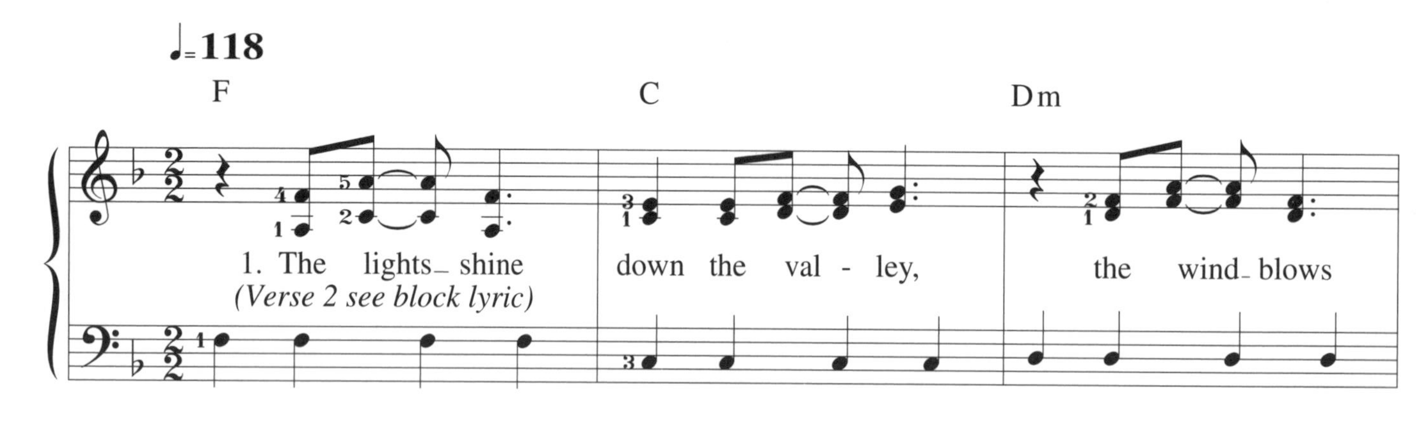

Dm
B♭
C
had to know_ she put me
right on my first mis - take.___
Sum-mer was-n't

Am
Dm
gone when I'd learned all she
had to show,_ she real - ly

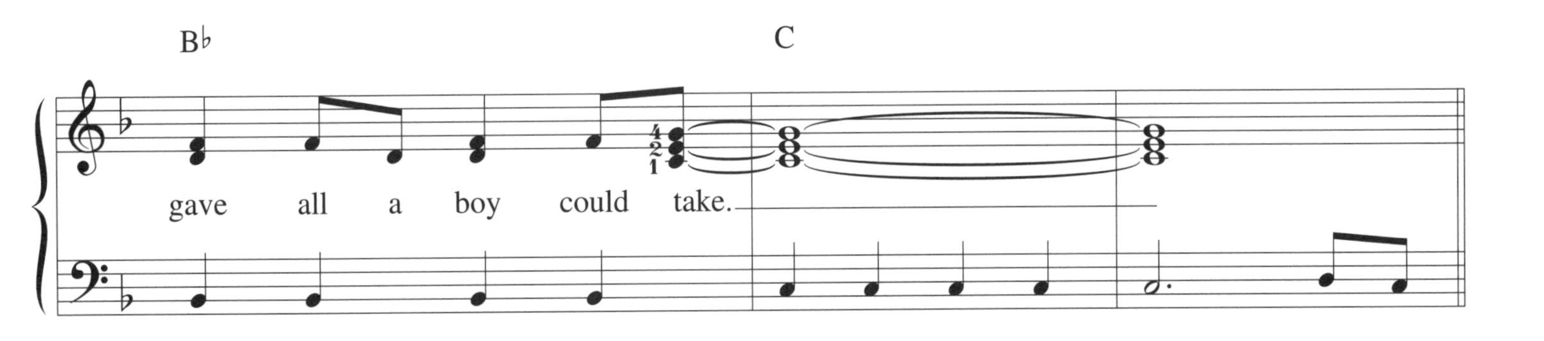
B♭
C
gave all a boy could take.

F
C
Dm
So now_ when
I feel lone - ly,
still look - ing for the

B♭6
F
C
one and on - ly,
that's_ when I wish I was
ly-ing in the arms of Ma-

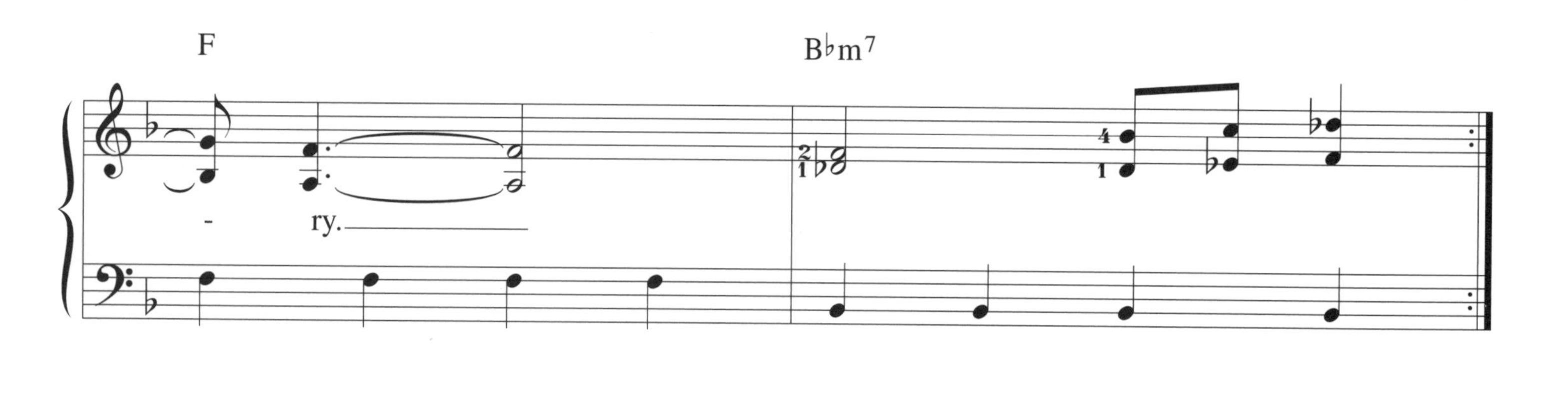

Verse 2:
She took the pains of boyhood
And turned them into feel good
Oh, and how I wish I was
Lying in the arms of Mary.

believe in me

Words & Music by
Martin Brannigan, Stephen Gately, Ronan Keating, Mark Taylor,
Paul Holgate & Ray Hedges.

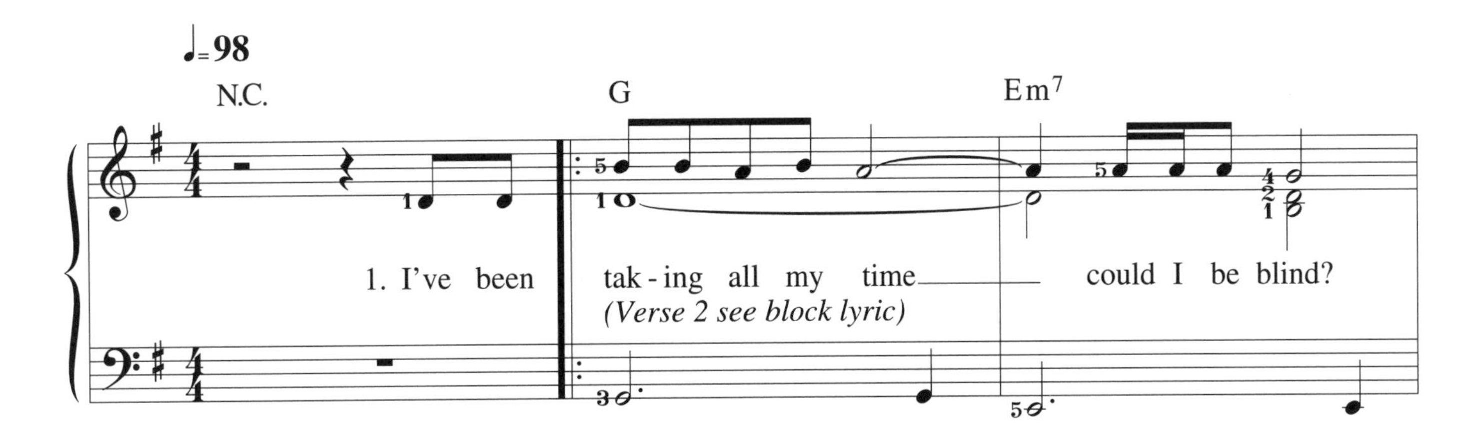

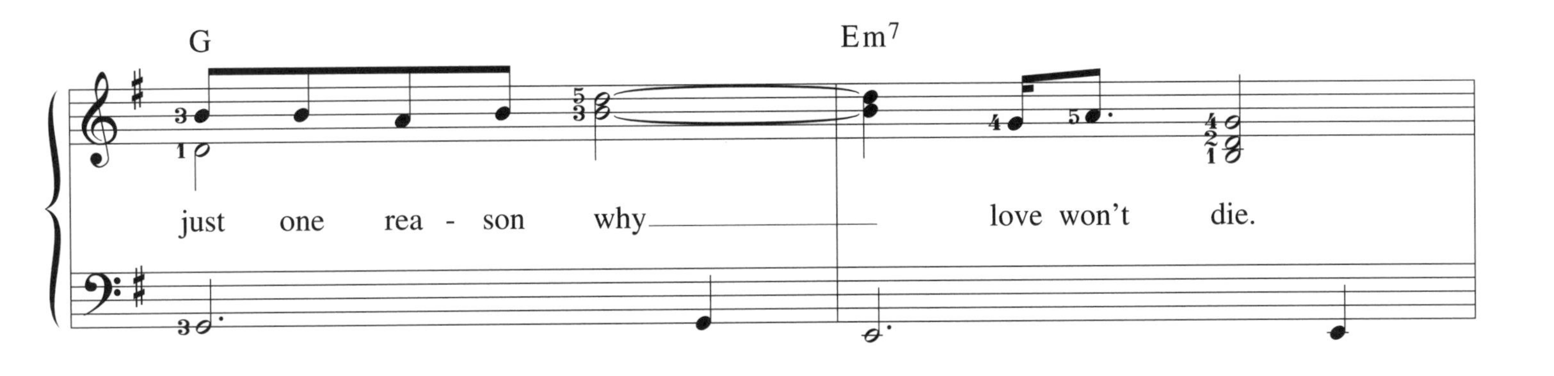

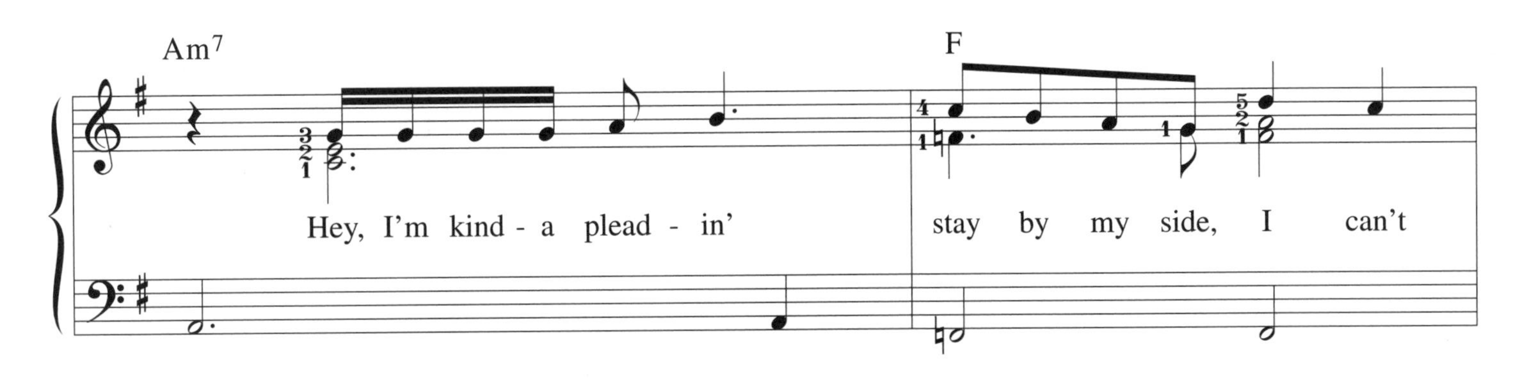

Gmaj7
Am7
Bm7
eat, can't sleep, you're the on - ly thing I care a - bout.

Em
Cmaj7
G
When you smile, you're so sweet, if

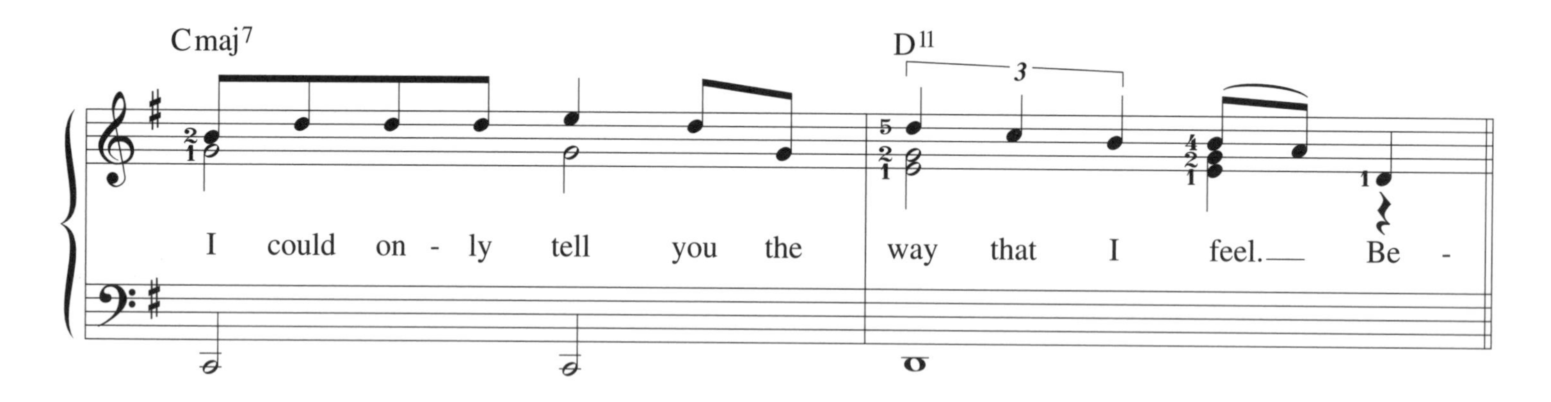
Cmaj7
D11
I could on - ly tell you the way that I feel. Be -

G
Em
Am7
-lieve in me, and you'll see that I'm

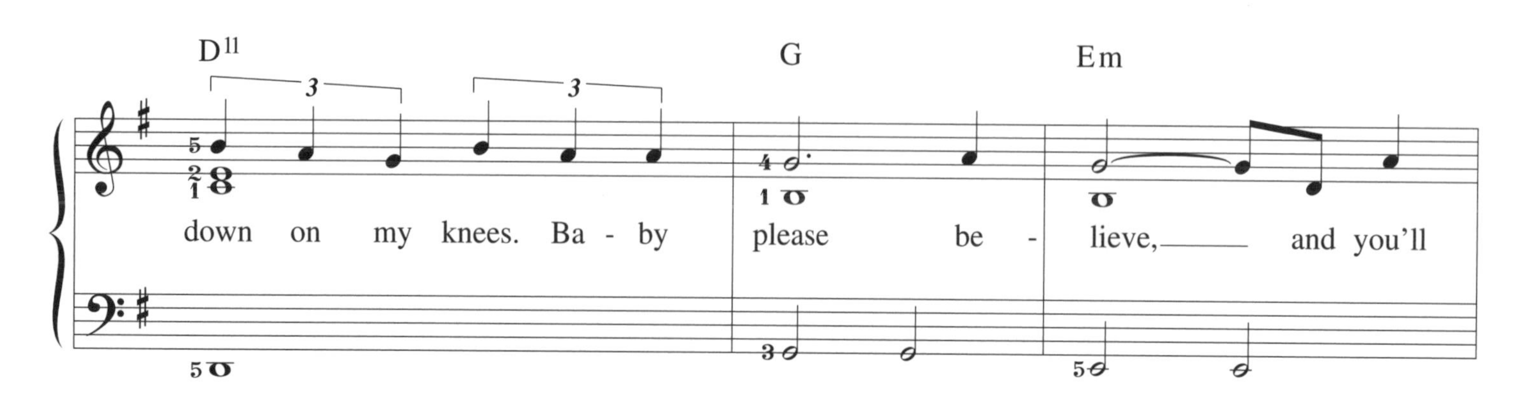
D11
G
Em
down on my knees. Ba - by please be - lieve, and you'll

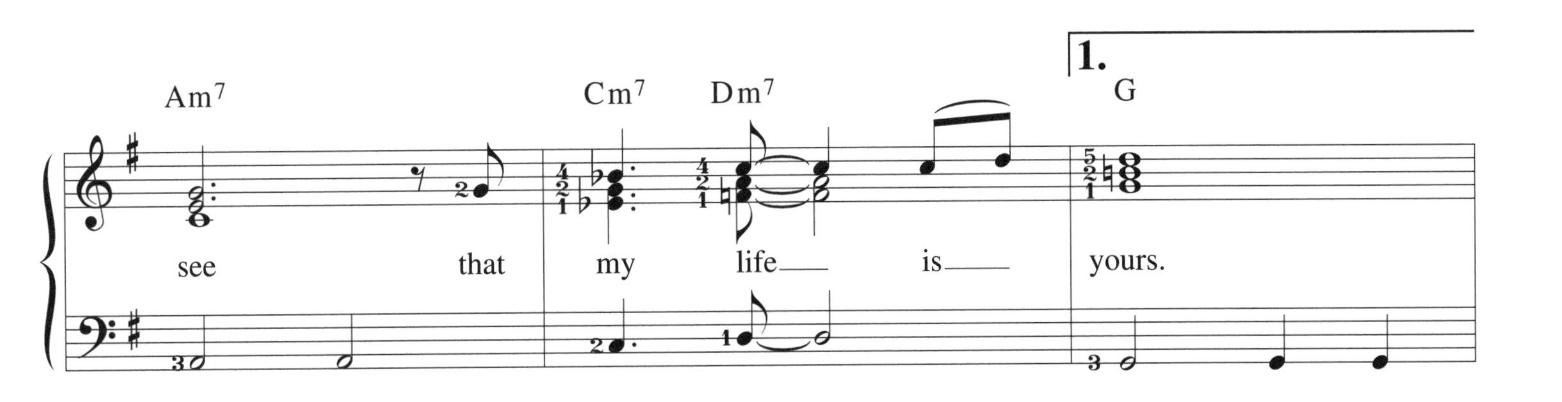

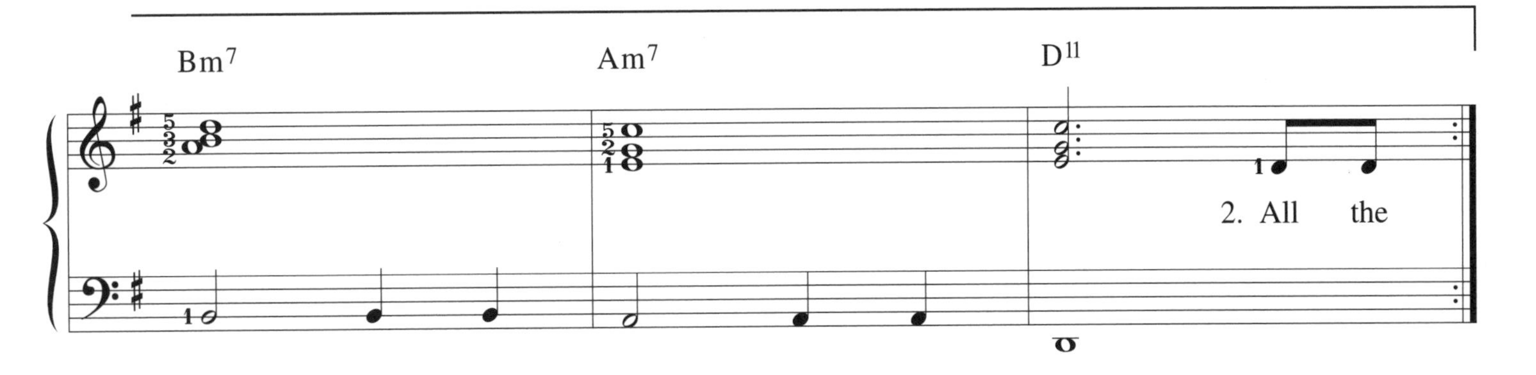

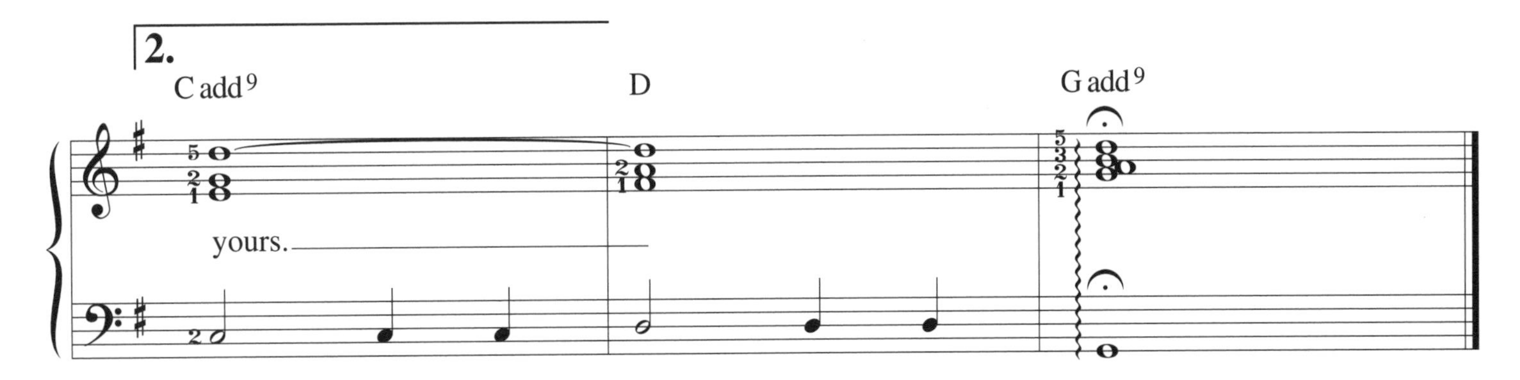

Verse 2:
All the mountains that we climb, day at a time
I promise you no heartache
Nothing left to hide
Swallow my pride
Guess you're not believing
I'm turning the tide.

'Cause I can't eat *etc.*

father and son

Words & Music by Cat Stevens.

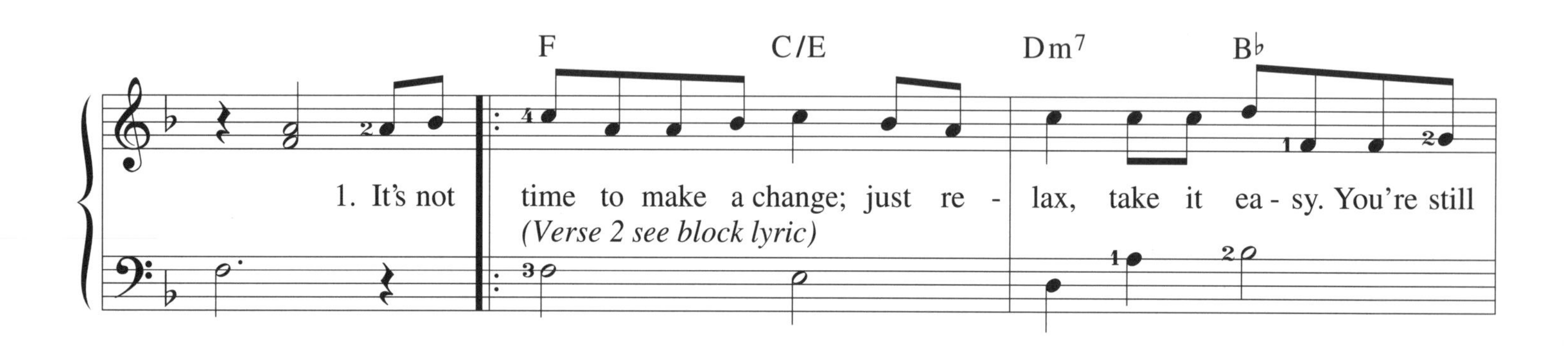

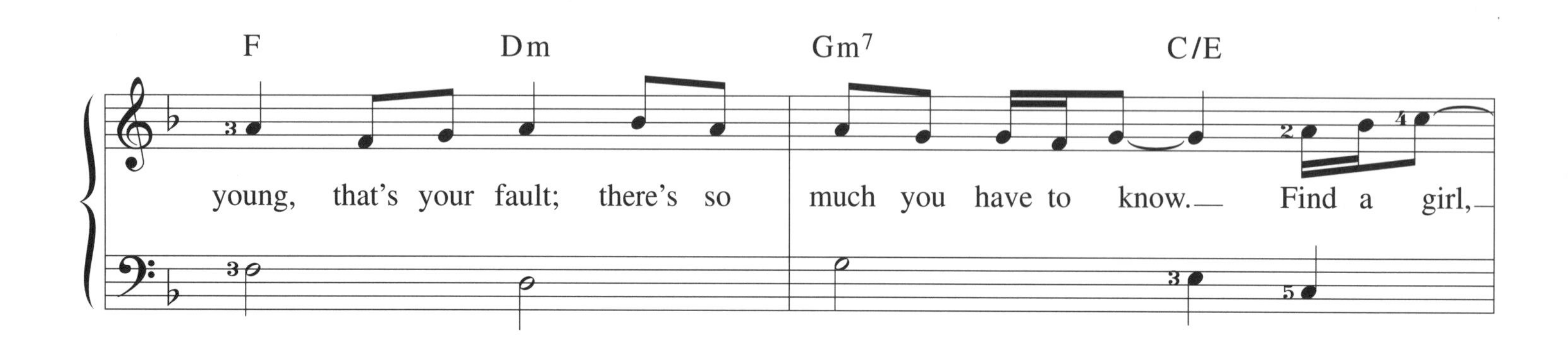

1.
F Dm Gm C
me: I am old but I'm hap - py. 2. I was
2.
F Dm C/E F B♭
still be here to - mor - row, but your dreams may not.
F C/E
3. How can I try to ex - plain? When I
(Verse 4 see block lyric)
Dm7 B♭ F Dm
do he turns a - way a - gain. Well, it's al - ways been the same, same old
Gm7 C F C/E
sto - ry. From the mo - ment I could talk, I was

To Coda
Dm7
B♭
F
Dm
or - dered to lis - ten; now there's a way, and I know that I

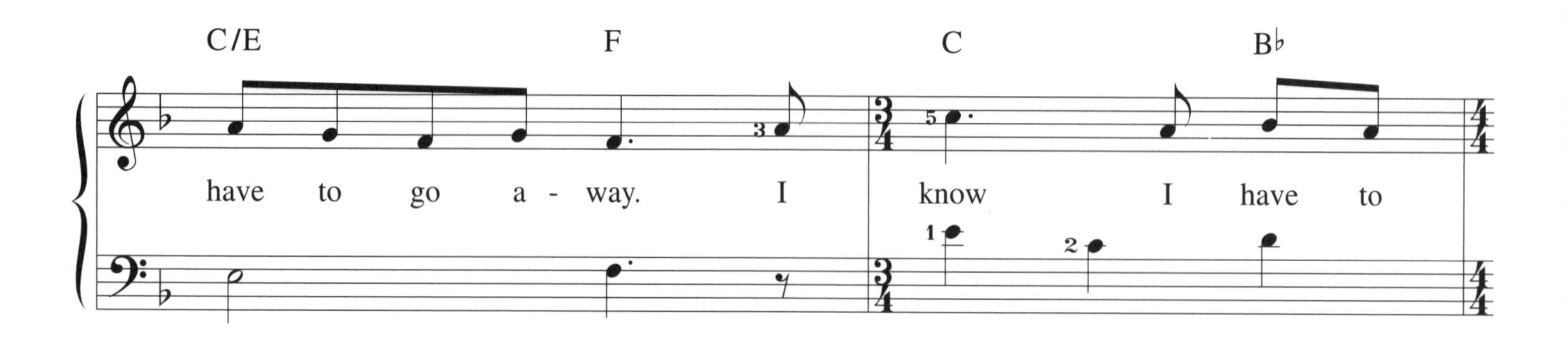
C/E
F
C
B♭
have to go a - way. I know I have to

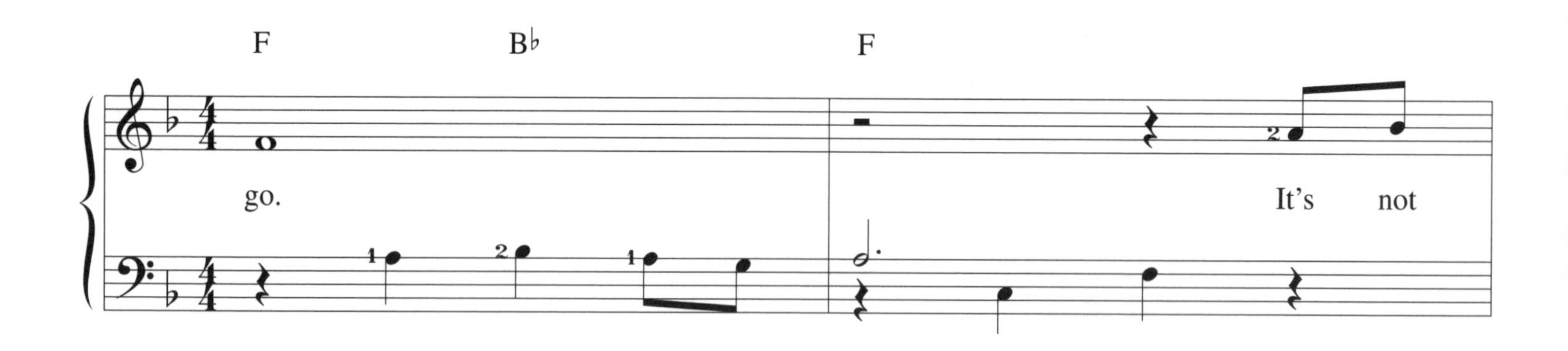
F
B♭
F
go. It's not

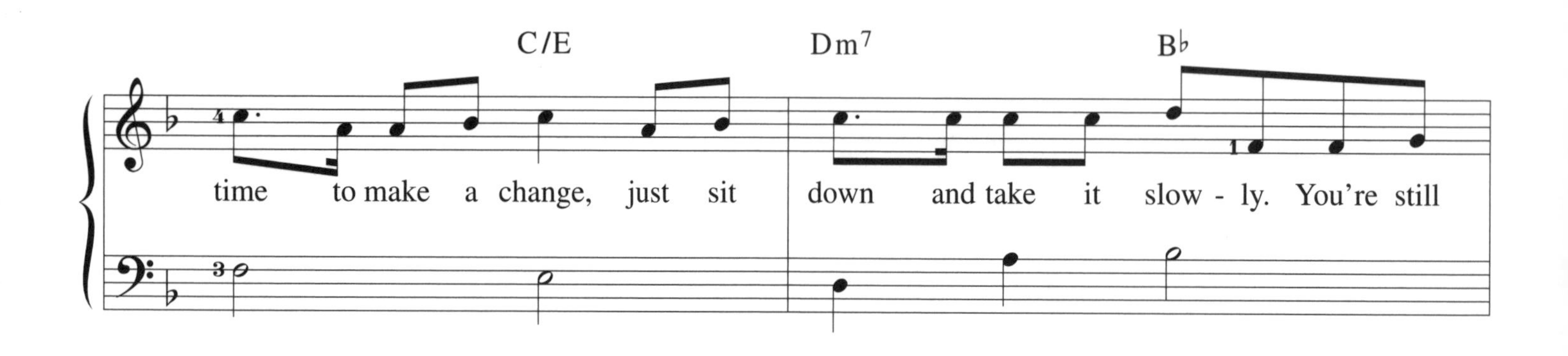
C/E
Dm7
B♭
time to make a change, just sit down and take it slow - ly. You're still

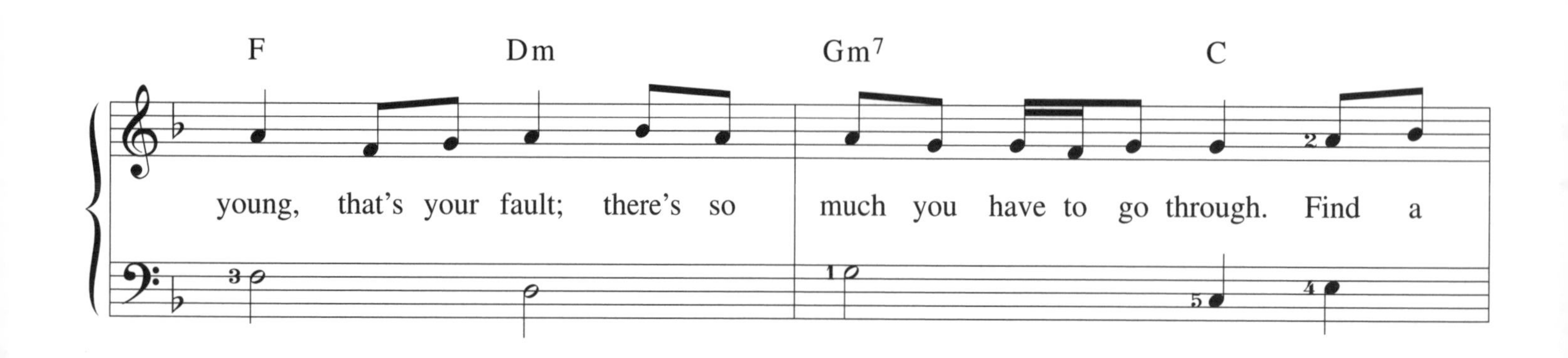
F
Dm
Gm7
C
young, that's your fault; there's so much you have to go through. Find a

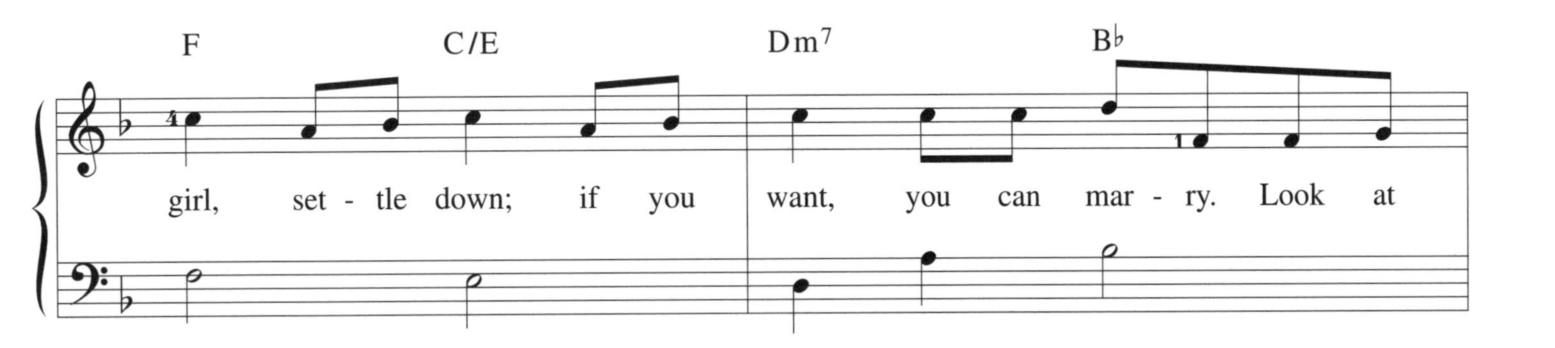

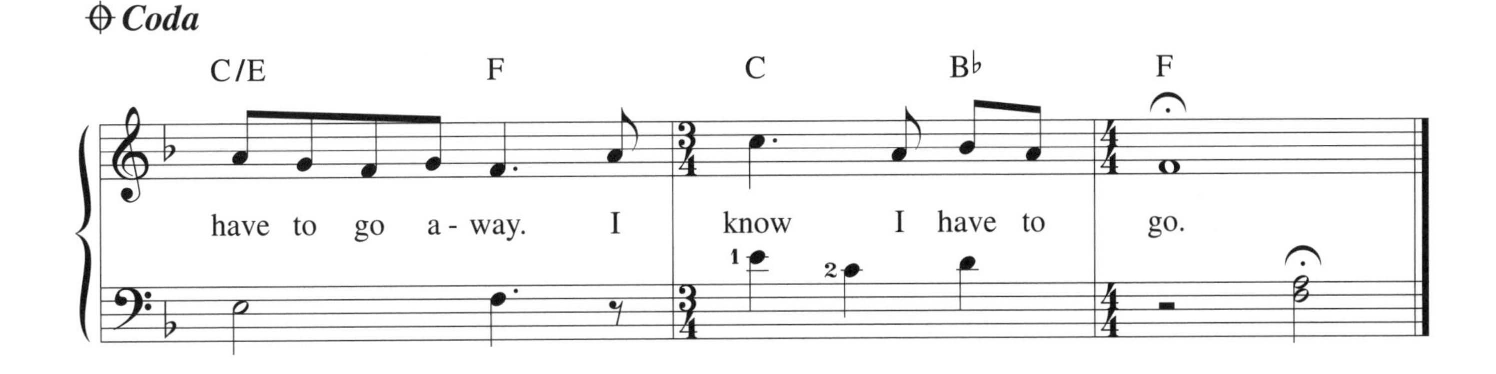

Verse 2:
I was once like you are now
And I know that it's not easy
To be calm when you've found something going on.
But take your time, think a lot
Think of everything you've got.
For you will still be here tomorrow
But your dreams may not.

Verse 4:
All the times that I've cried
Keeping all the things I knew inside
And it's hard, but it's harder to ignore it.
If they were right I'd agree
But it's them they know, not me
Now there's a way, and I know
That I have to go away.
I know I have to go.

love me for a reason

Words & Music by
John Bristol, Wade Brown Jr & David Jones Jr.

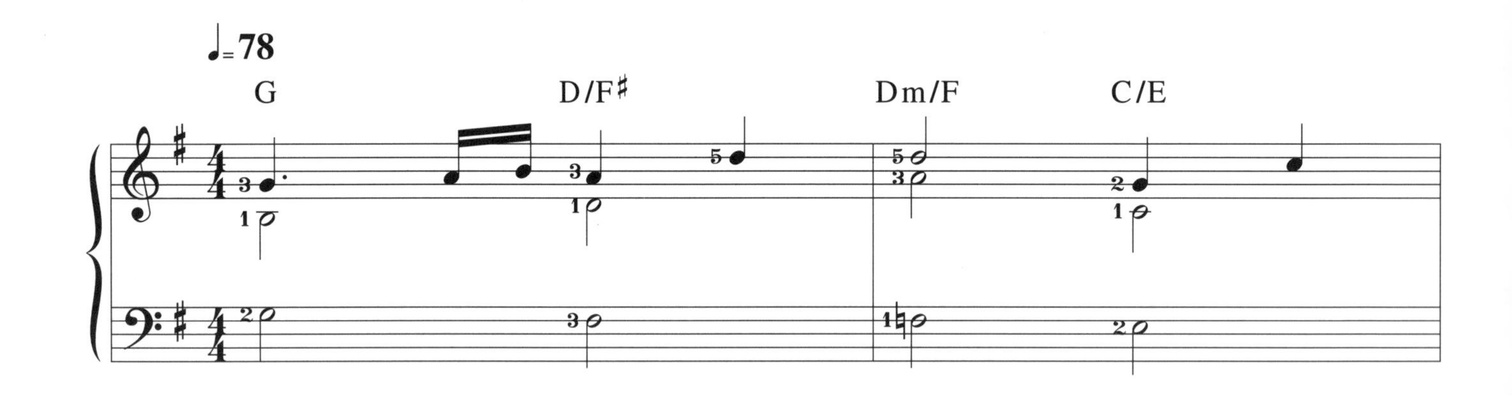

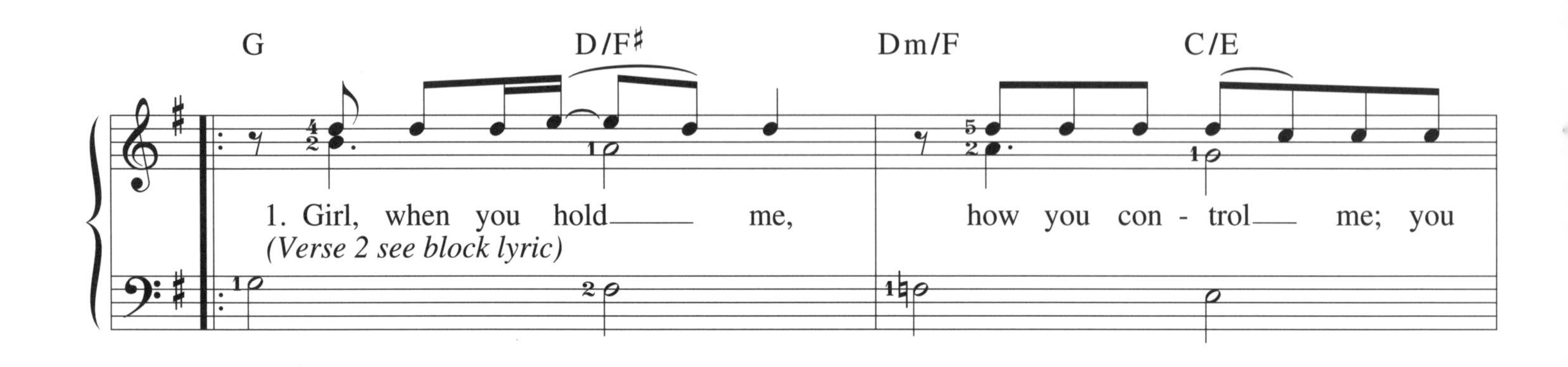

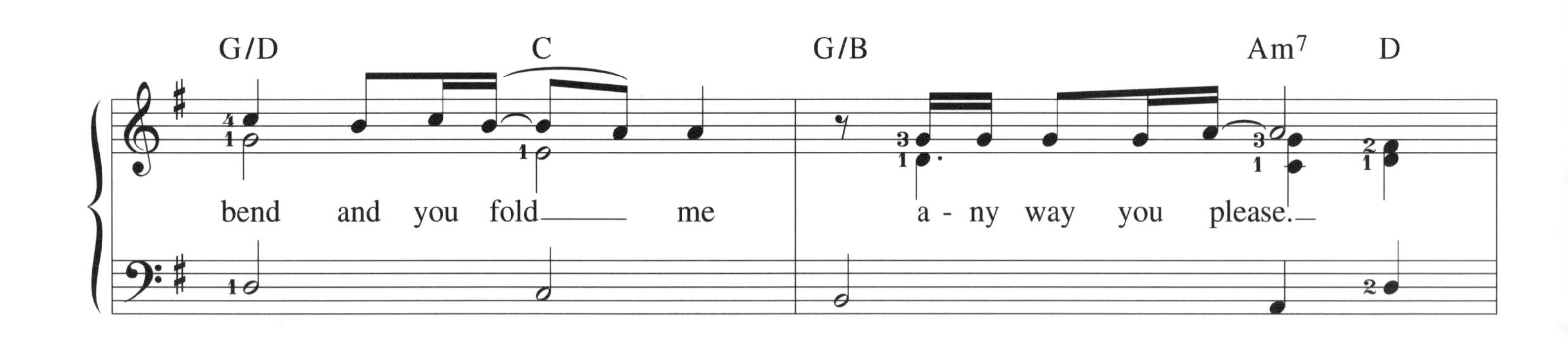

G
D/F♯
Dm/F
C/E
It must be ea - sy for you,
the love-ly things that you do are

G/D
C
G/D
Dsus4
D
just a pas - time for you,
I could nev - er be.

Bm7
Em9
Am7
C
D
And I nev - er know, girl,
if I should stay or go,
'cos the games

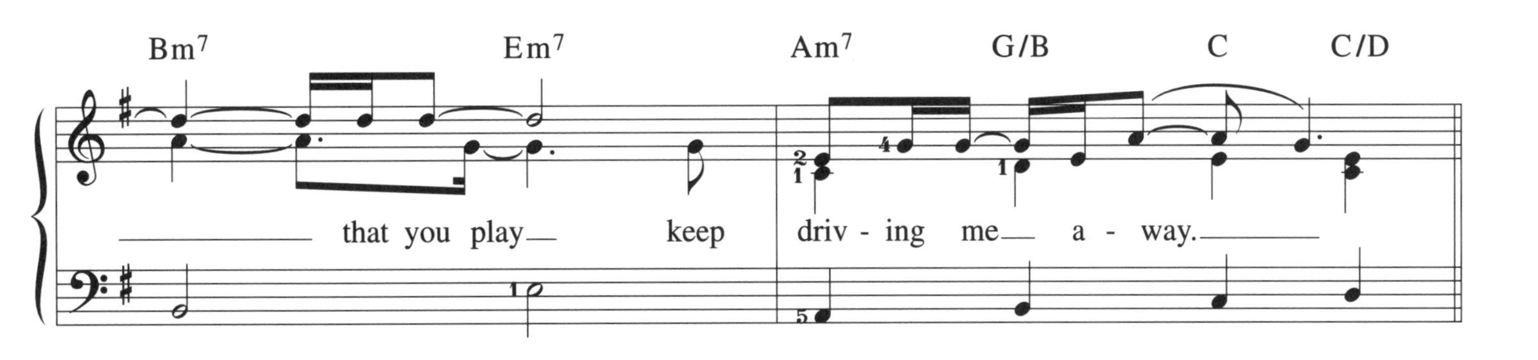
Bm7
Em7
Am7
G/B
C
C/D
that you play keep
driv - ing me a - way.

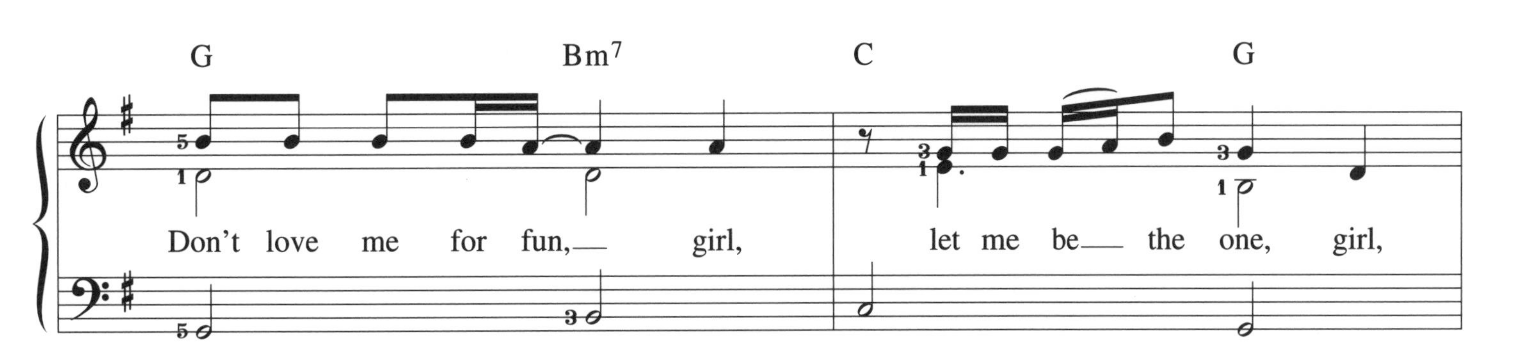
G
Bm7
C
G
Don't love me for fun, girl,
let me be the one, girl,

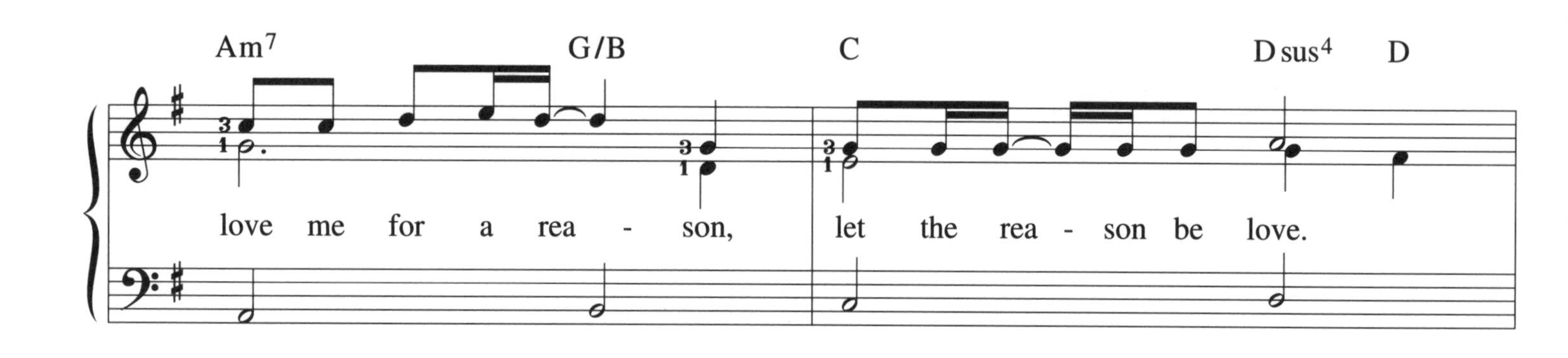
Am7 G/B C Dsus4 D
love me for a rea - son, let the rea - son be love.

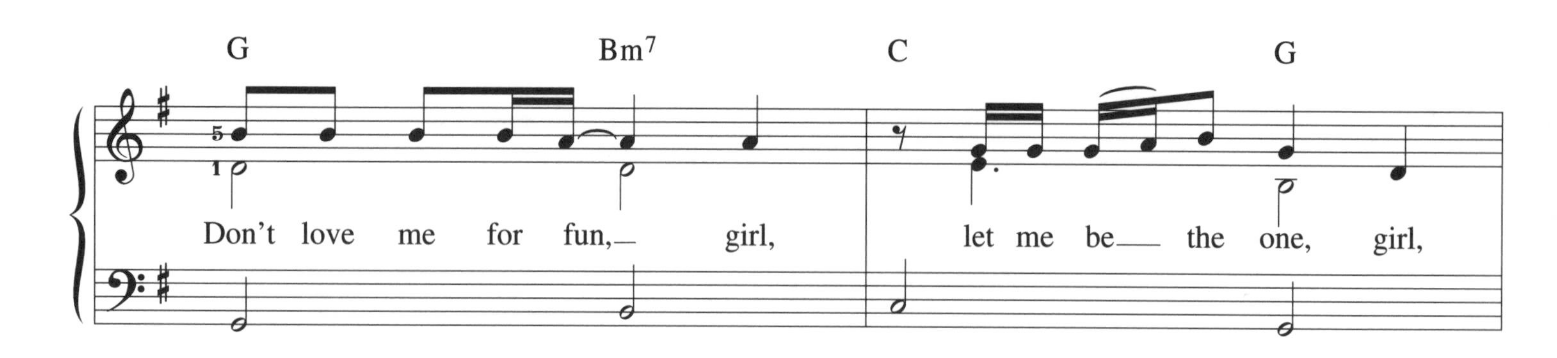
G Bm7 C G
Don't love me for fun, girl, let me be the one, girl,

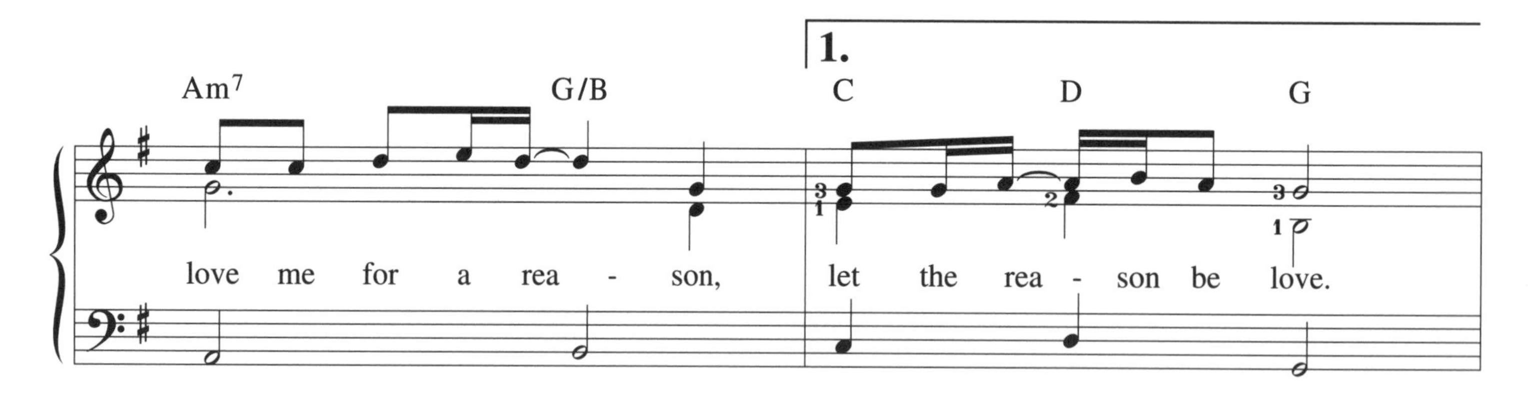
1.
Am7 G/B C D G
love me for a rea - son, let the rea - son be love.

C/D G/D C G D

2.
C D G F9 G Bm7
let the rea - son be love. Don't love me for fun, girl

Verse 2:
Kisses and caresses are only minor tests, babe
Of love needs and stresses between a woman and a man.
So if love everlasting isn't what you're asking
I'll have to pass, girl: I'm proud to take a stand.
I can't continue guessing, because it's only messing
With my pride and my mind.
So write down this time to time:

Don't love me for fun, girl *etc.*

key to my life

Words & Music by
Martin Brannigan, Stephen Gately, Ronan Keating,
Michael Graham, & Ray Hedges.

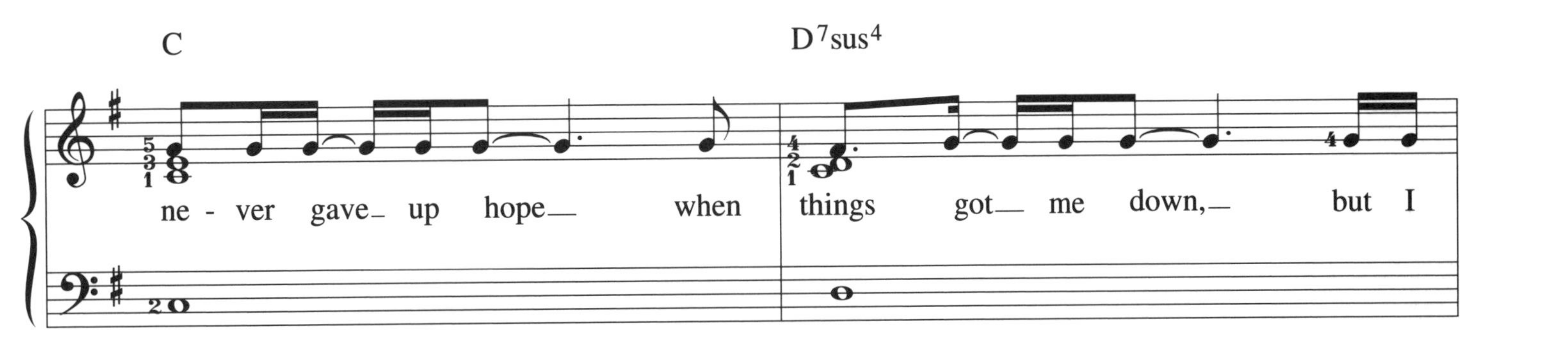
C
D7sus4
ne - ver gave up hope when things got me down, but I

C
D
G
just bit on my lip and my face be - gan to frown. 'Cos

C add9
D
that was just my pride, and I've no - thing left to hide, and

Am7
D
now the way is clear, and all I want to say is:

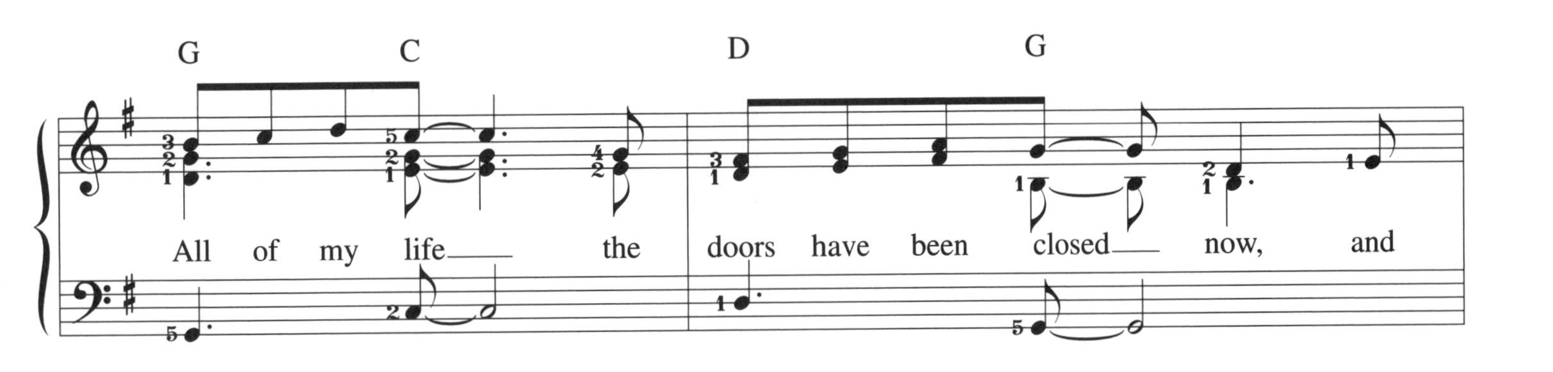
G
C
D
G
All of my life the doors have been closed now, and

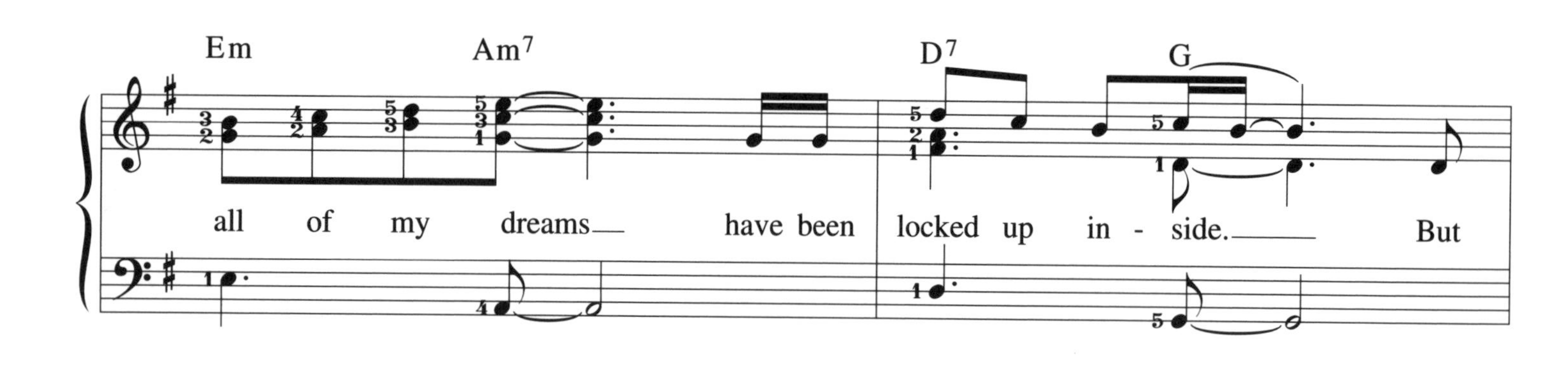
Em
Am7
D7
G
all of my dreams have been locked up in - side. But

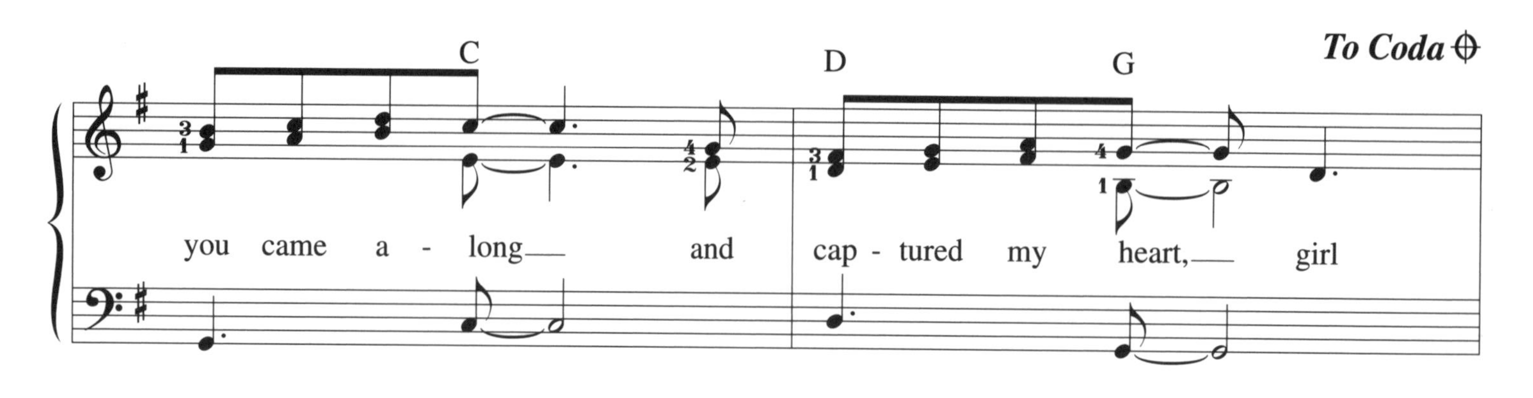
To Coda
C
D
G
you came a - long and cap - tured my heart, girl

C
D
G7
you're the key to my life.

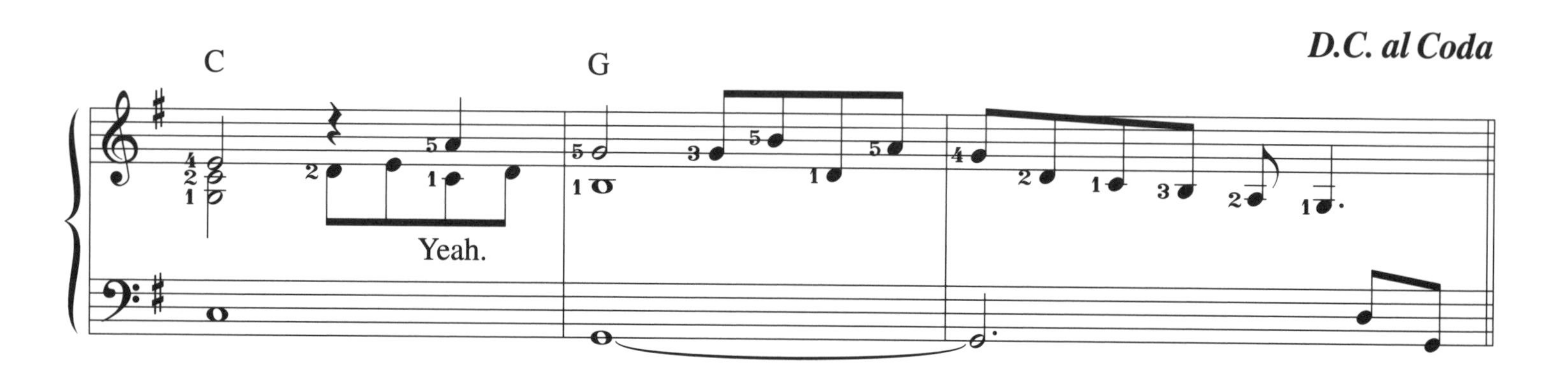
D.C. al Coda
C
G
Yeah.

Coda
C
D
F add9
you're the key to my life.
Girl, you know that I feel for you

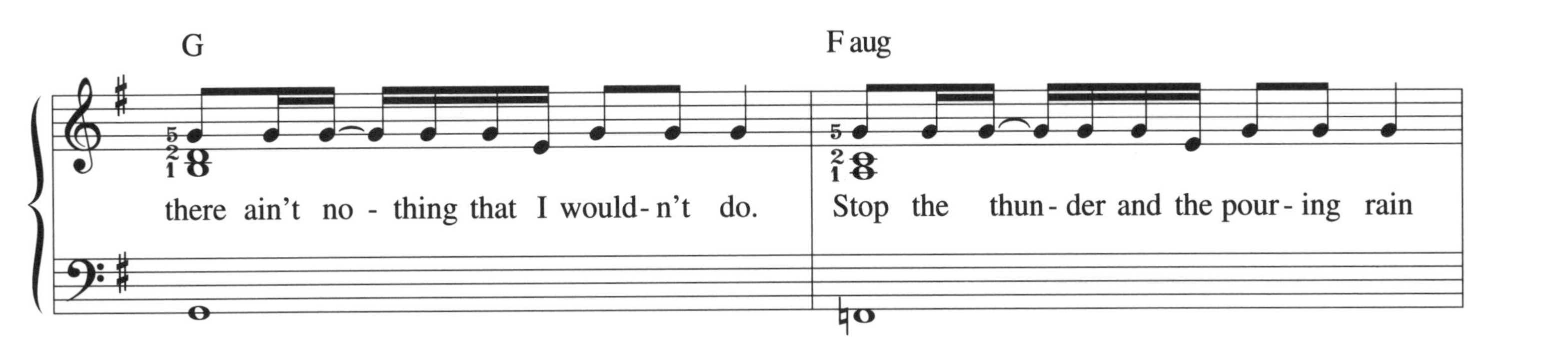
G
F aug
there ain't no - thing that I would-n't do.
Stop the thun-der and the pour-ing rain

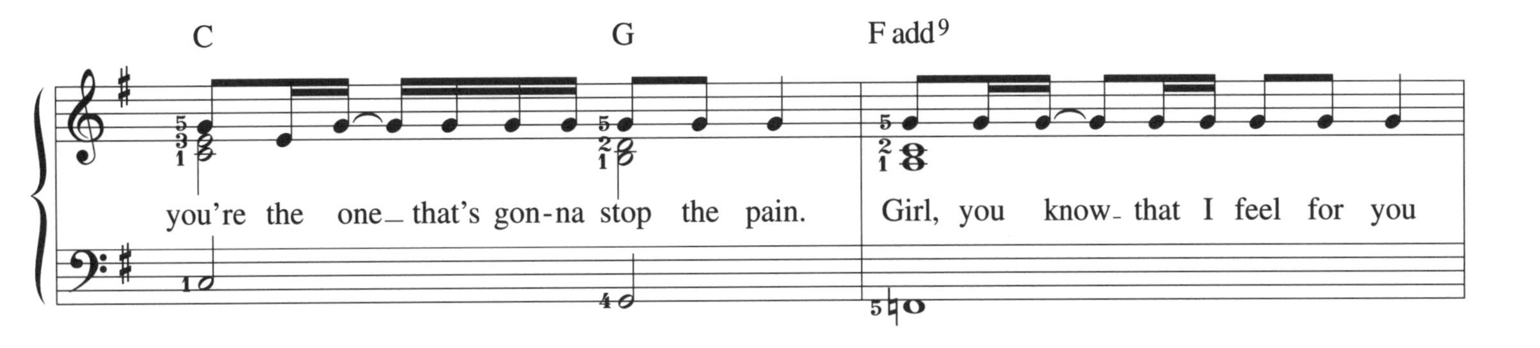
C
G
F add9
you're the one that's gon-na stop the pain.
Girl, you know that I feel for you

G
C
there ain't no - thing that I would-n't do.
Stop the thun-der and the pour-ing rain,

D
G
C
lis - ten to me, can't you hear what I say?
All of my life the

D
G
Em
Am7
doors have been closed now, and
all of my dreams have been

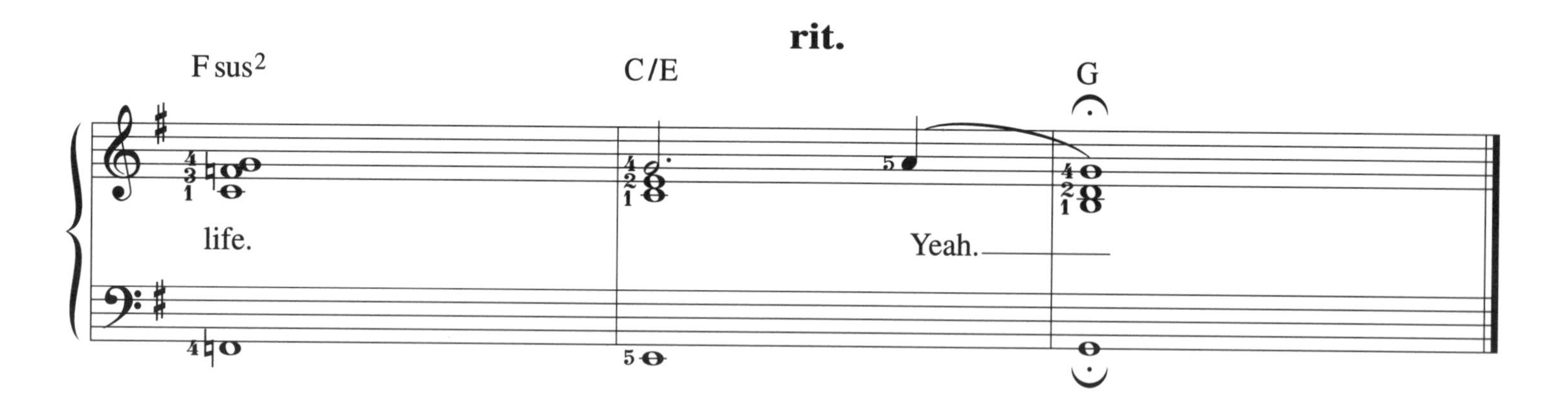

Verse 2:
Stain on the desktop where coffee cup lay
And memories of you forever will stay
And the scent of your perfume
And the smile on your face will remain.

Verse 3:
Year after year, was blaming myself
For what I'd done; just thought of myself.
I know that you'll understand
This was all my own fault – don't go away.

when all is said and done

Words & Music by
Martin Brannigan, Stephen Gately, Ronan Keating, Michael Graham,
Shane Lynch, Keith Duffy & Ray Hedges.

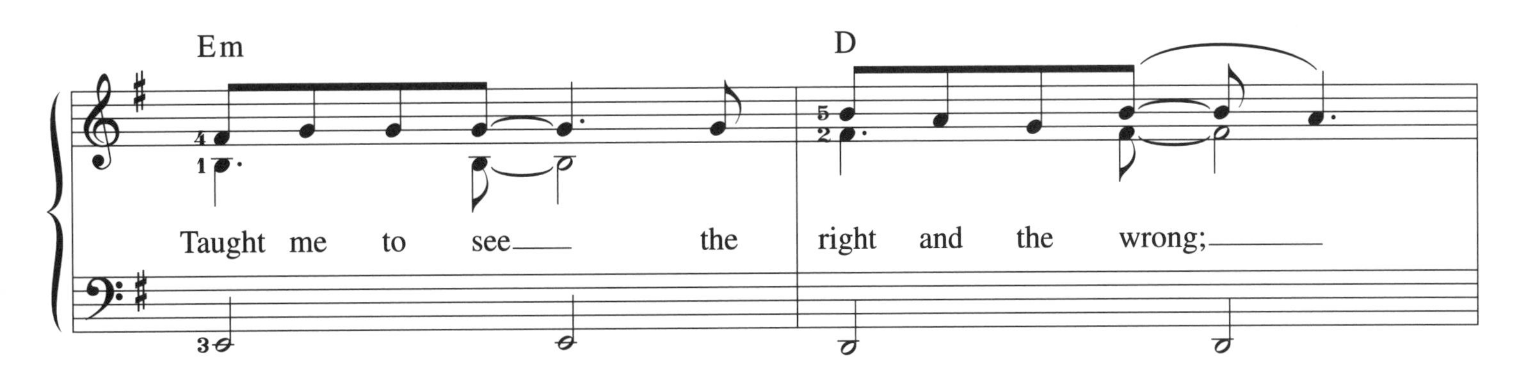

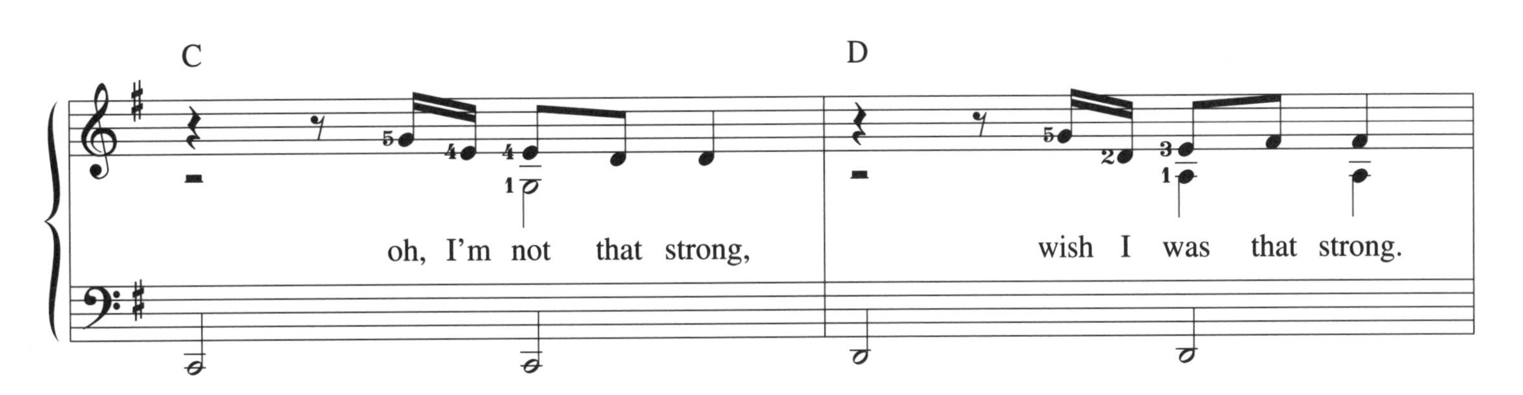

Em
D
You've been good to me,
tend-ing my ev - 'ry
C
Em
D
need.
Just look what I am,
D/F♯
E/G♯
F/A
G/G
can't you see, it's you in me?
C
F
When all is said and done,
C
G
look be - fore you,
I'm your son.

Verse 2:
Now I'm a man, time has gone fast;
I didn't want it to, I didn't want it to.
Went on my way like a crazy young fool;
I never wanted to, I never wanted to.

You've been good *etc.*

a different beat

Words & Music by
Martin Brannigan, Stephen Gately, Ronan Keating,
Shane Lynch, Keith Duffy & Ray Hedges.

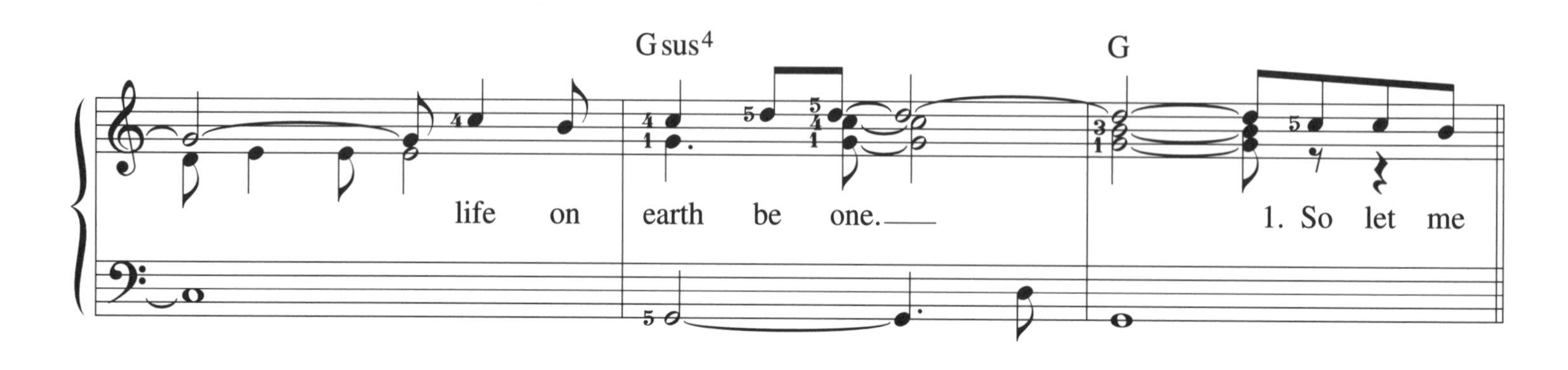

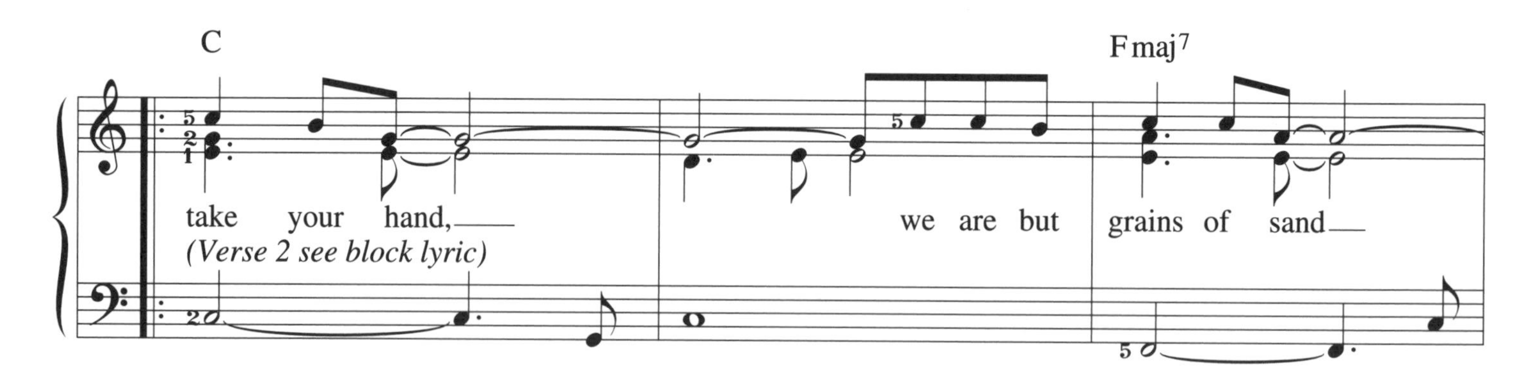

C
born through the winds of time,
G sus4
G
gi - ven a spe - cial sign.
So
F
G
let's take a stand and look a - round us now,
peo - ple.
So
F
G
let's take a stand and look a - round us now,
peo - ple.
Ee -
C
F
Am7
- yea oh, ee - yea oh, ee - yea oh, by - yah.

G C F
Ee - yea oh, ee - yea oh, ee -
Am7 1. G 2. G
- yea oh, by - yah. 2. Hu - ma - ni -
C/E F G Am
I've seen the rain fall in Af - ri - ca,
C/E F G C
I've touched the snows of A - las - ka,
C/E F G Am
I've felt the mists of Ni - a - ga - ra, now I be -

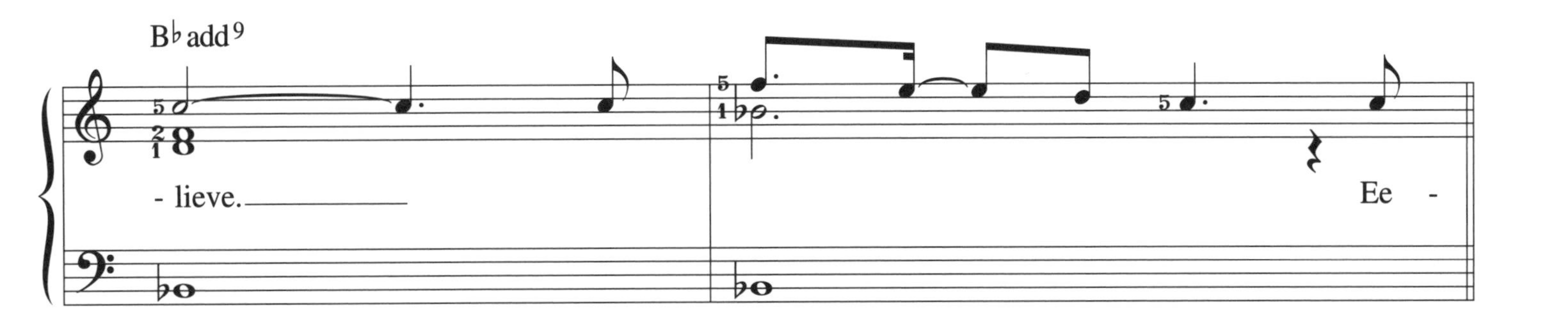

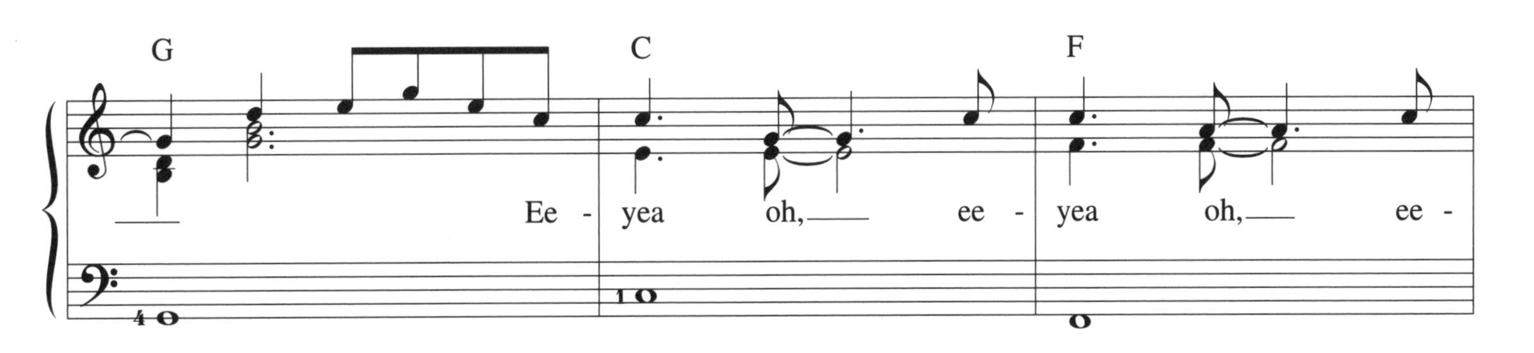

Verse 2:
Humanity has lost face
Let's understand it's grace
Each day, one at a time
Each life, including mine.

Let's take a stand and look around us now
People
So let's take a stand and look around us now
People, oh people, oh people.

crying in the night

Words & Music by
Martin Brannigan, Stephen Gately, Ronan Keating,
Shane Lynch & Ray Hedges.

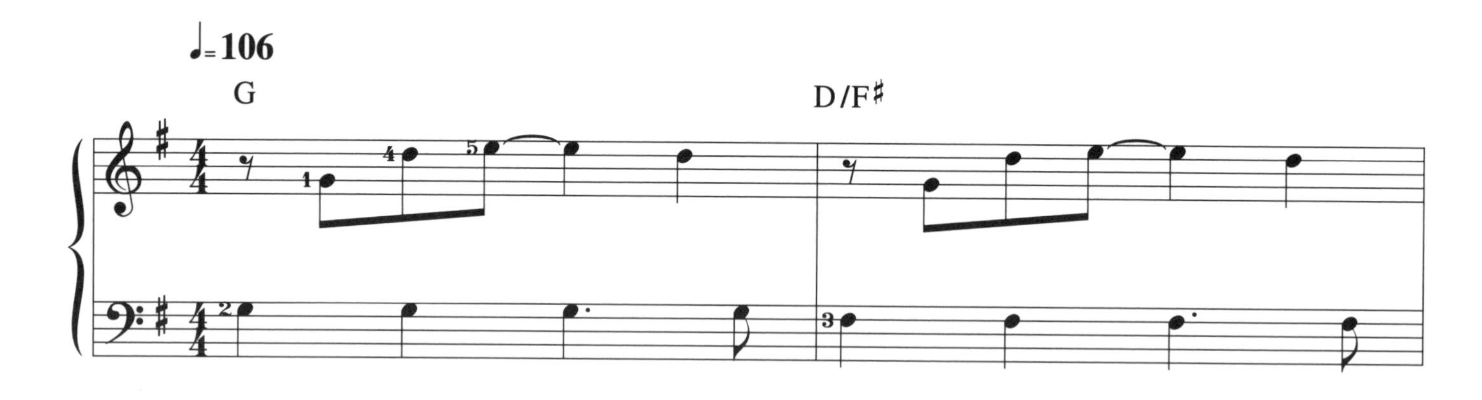

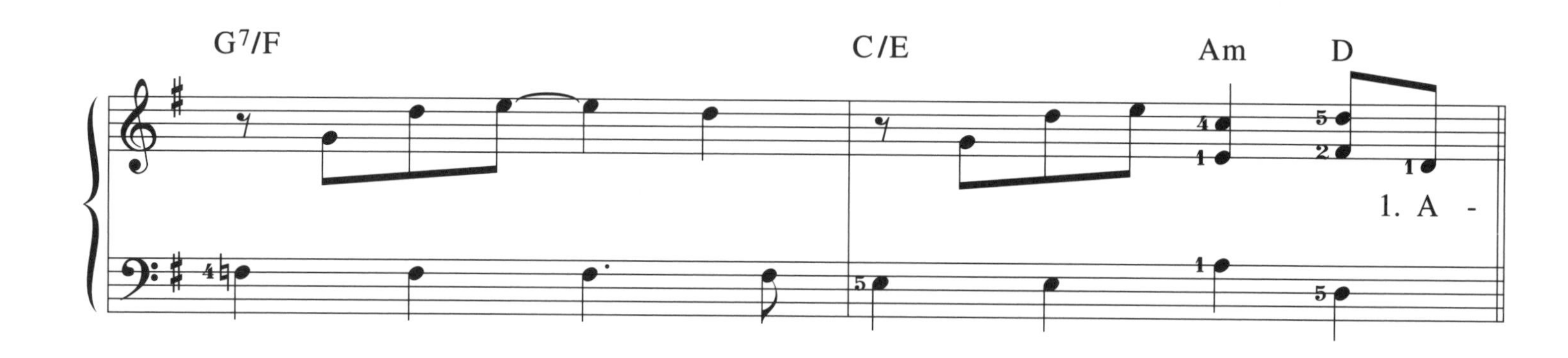

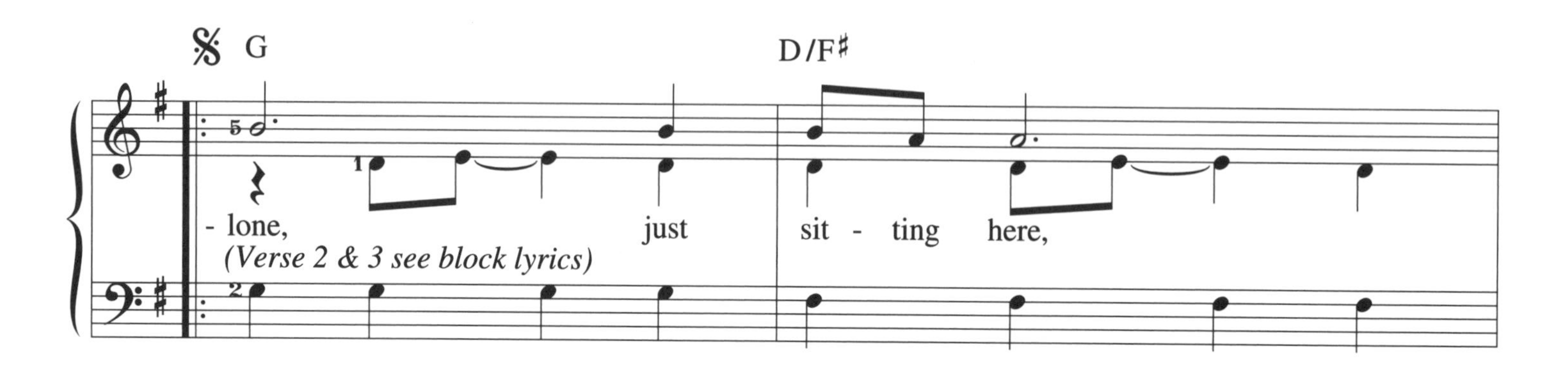

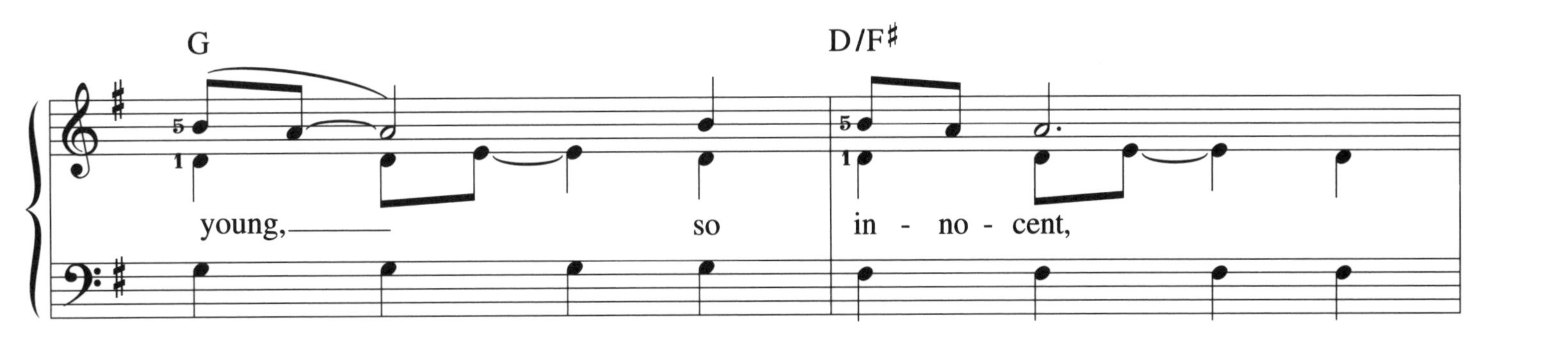
G
D/F♯
young, so in - no - cent,

G7/F
C/E
with out a care in the world. You're

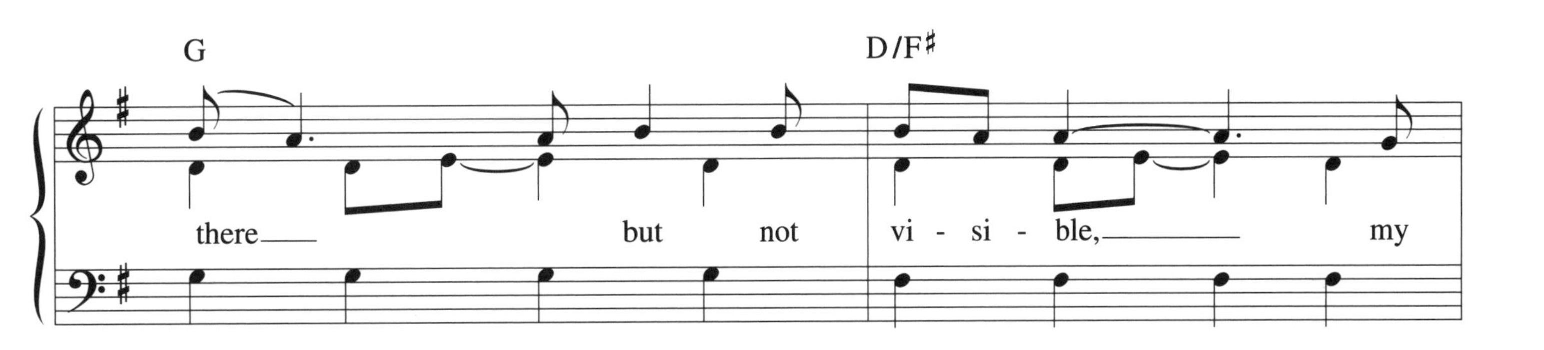
G
D/F♯
there but not vi - si - ble, my

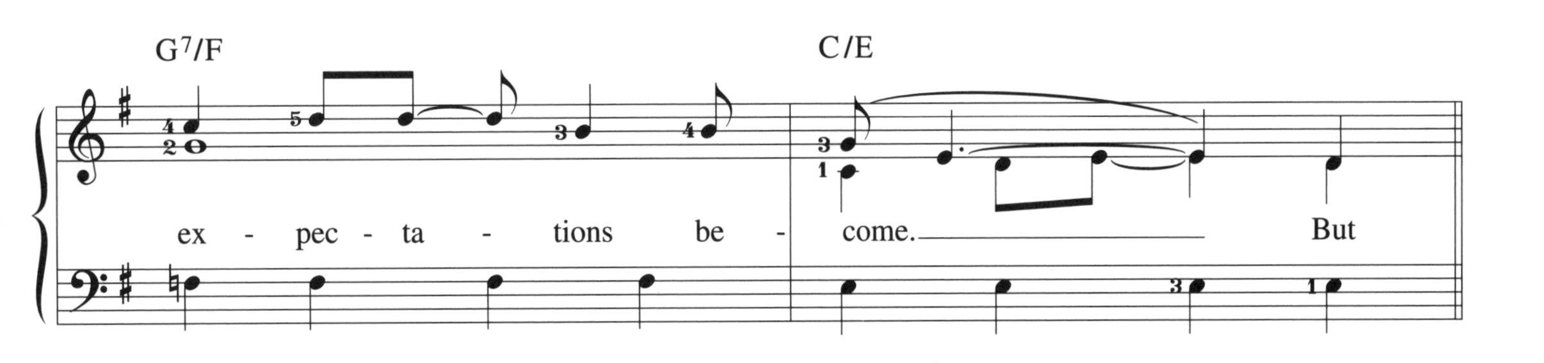
G7/F
C/E
ex - pec - ta - tions be - come. But

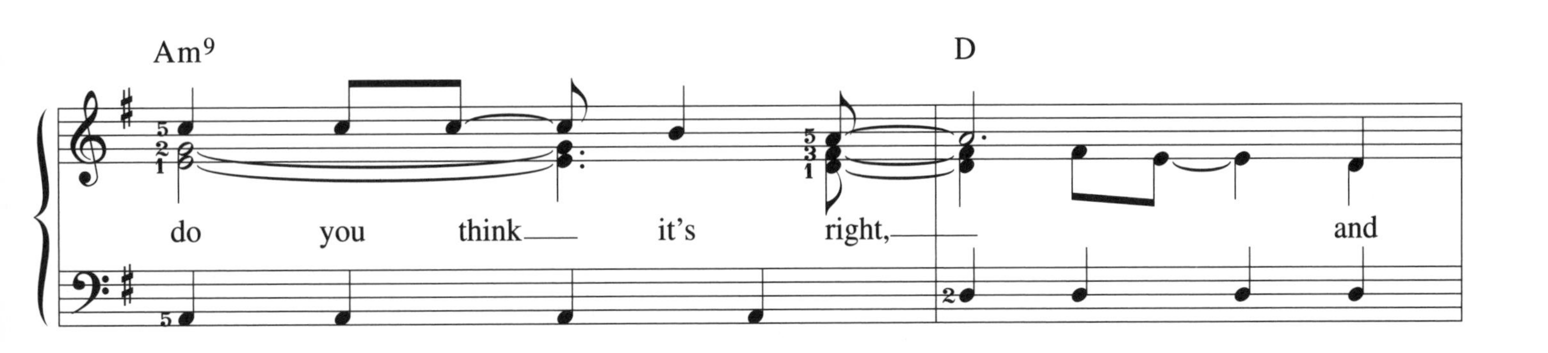
Am9
D
do you think it's right, and

Am9
D
do you think it's right,
cry - ing in the

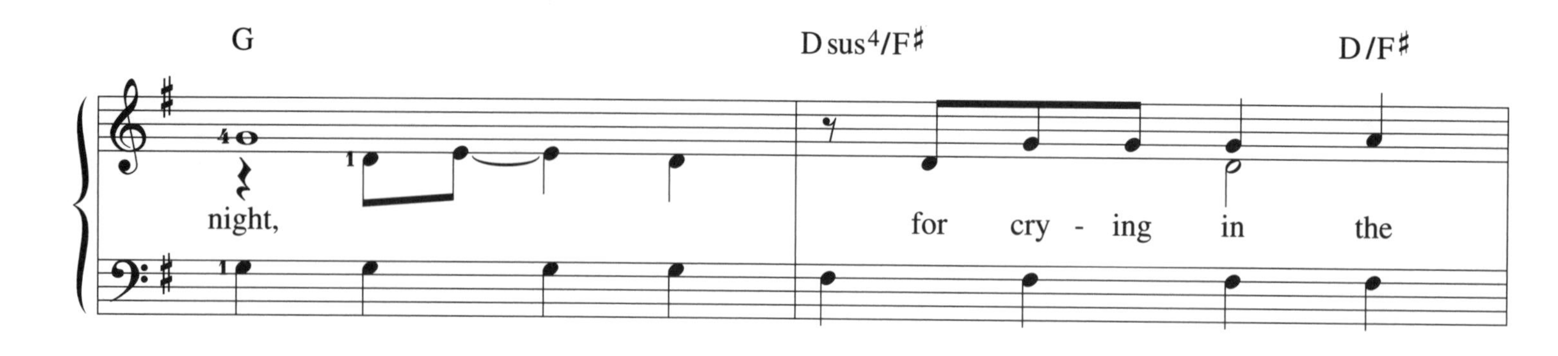
G
Dsus4/F♯
D/F♯
night,
for cry - ing in the

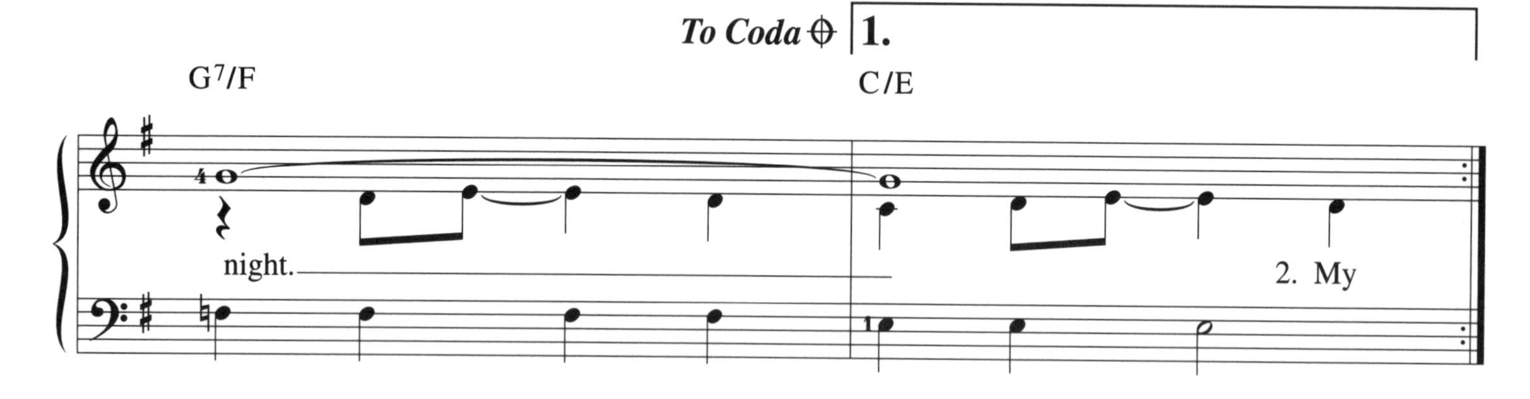
To Coda
1.
G7/F
C/E
night.
2. My

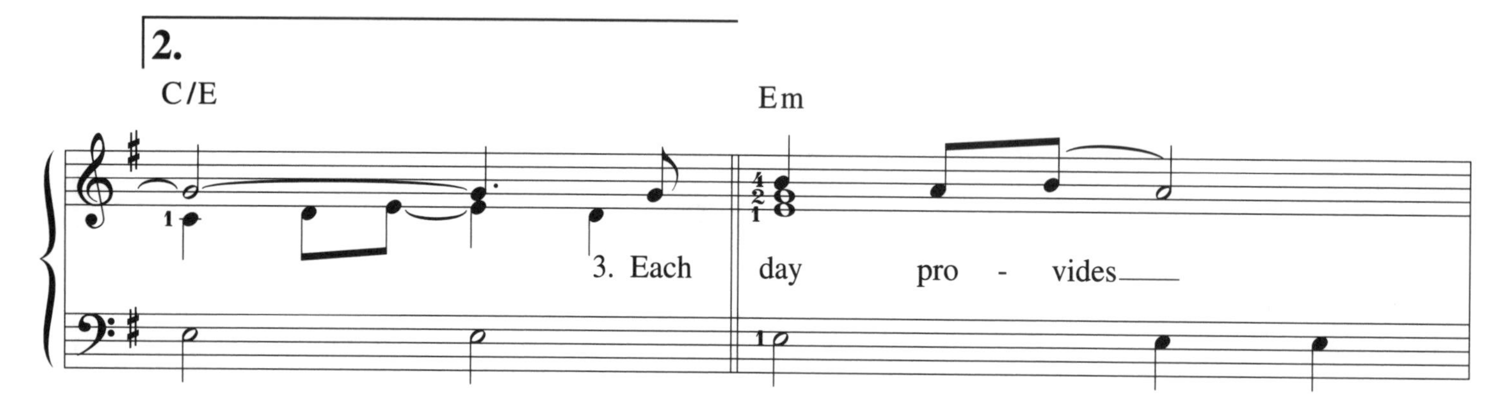
2.
C/E
Em
3. Each
day pro - vides

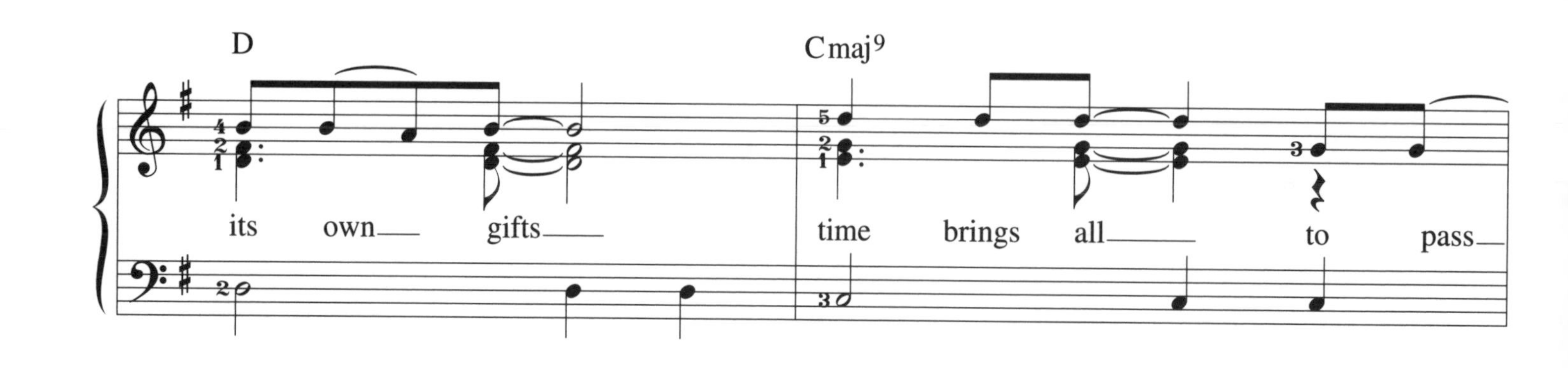
D
Cmaj9
its own gifts
time brings all to pass

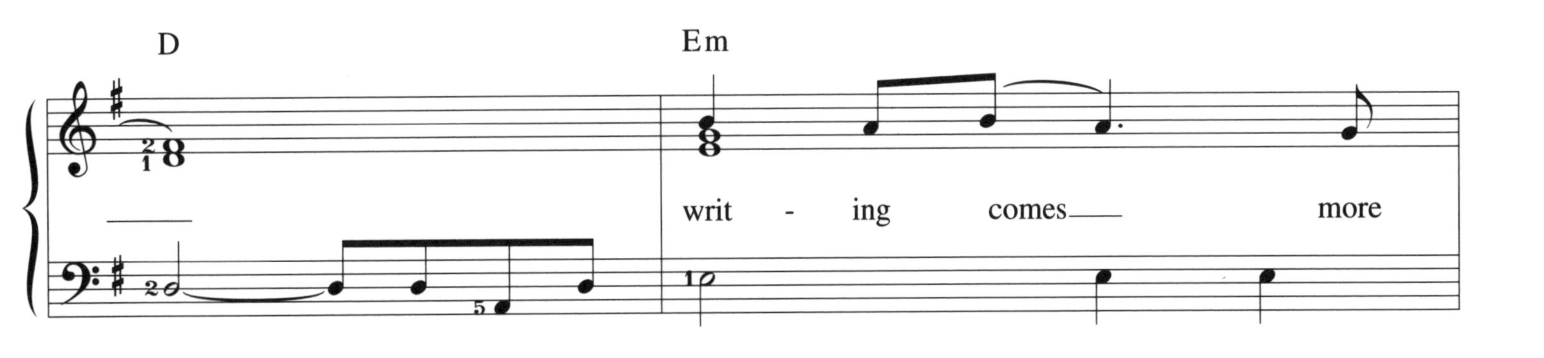

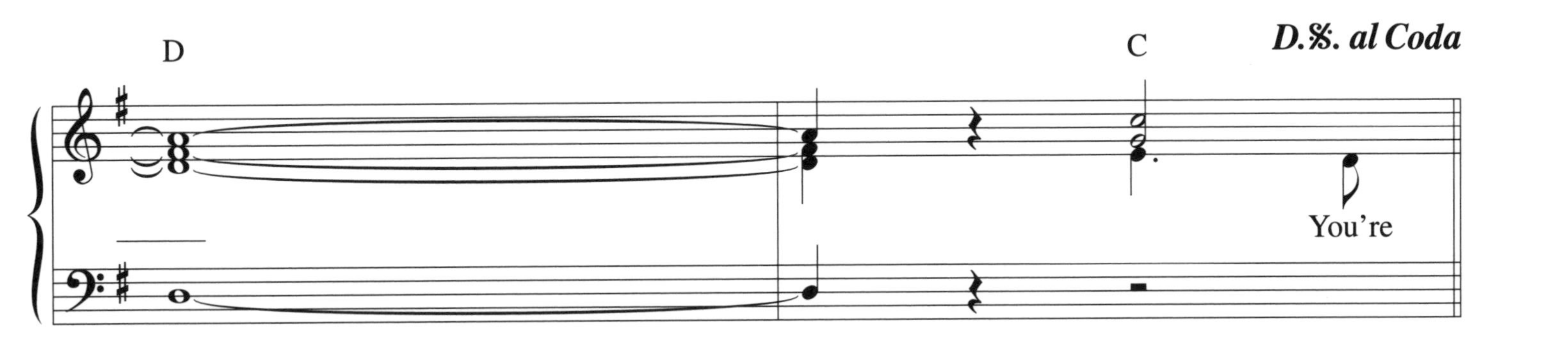

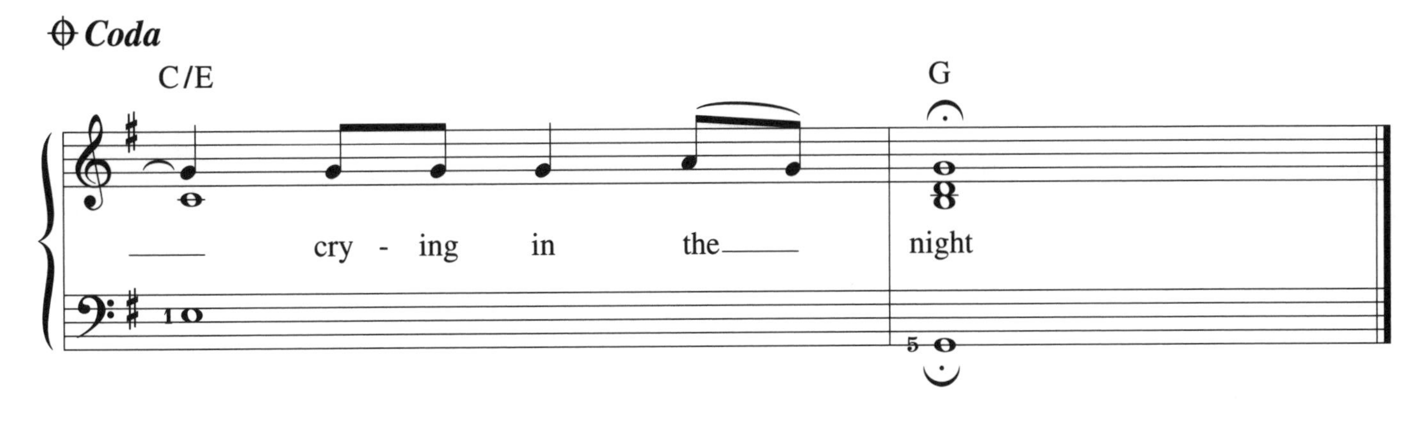

Verse 2:
My road was different
There's so much that you have to learn
A little hand in mine
And all the smiles and laughter is fine.
Wherever I'll be, land or sea
I will care for thee.

Verse 3:
You're young, you're beautiful
Have no enemy but time
And in time, those who take time
When time does last.
For time is no time
When time is passed.

don't stop looking for love

Words & Music by
Billy Mann & Brett Laurence.

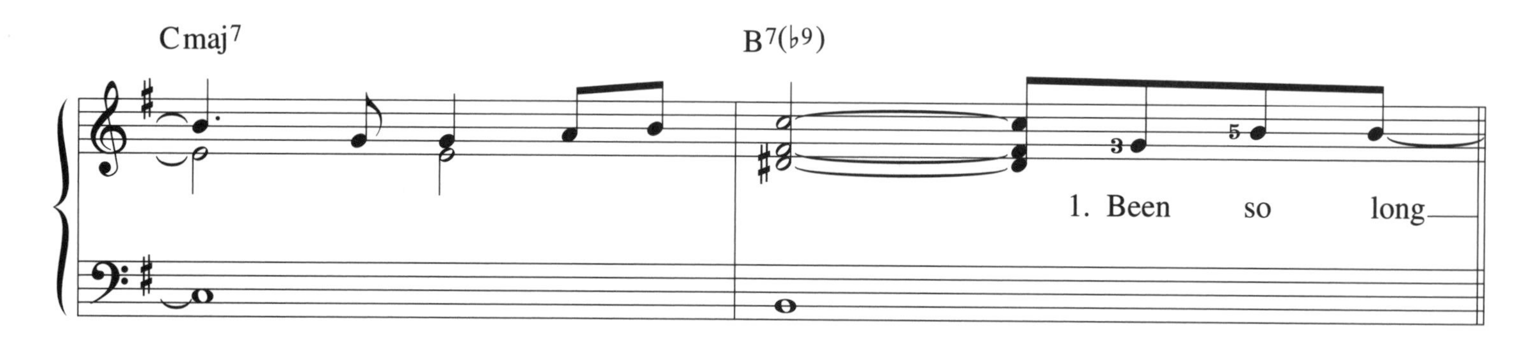

Bm7
Em9
Am11
I looked in your eyes, so beau - ti - ful and strong,

D/F♯
B7
Em7
girl, where did you come from? As

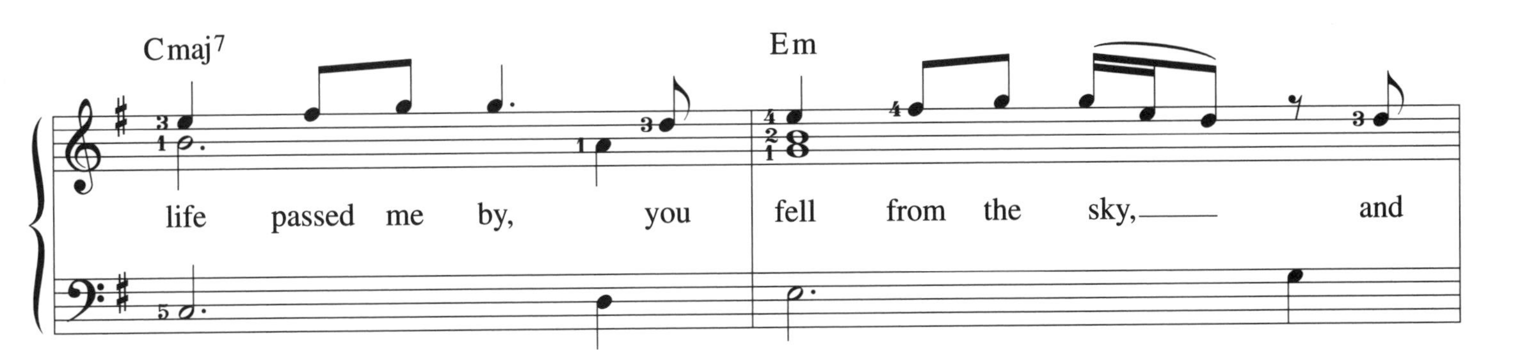
Cmaj7
Em
life passed me by, you fell from the sky, and

Am9
D7sus4
D9
I could hear you say:

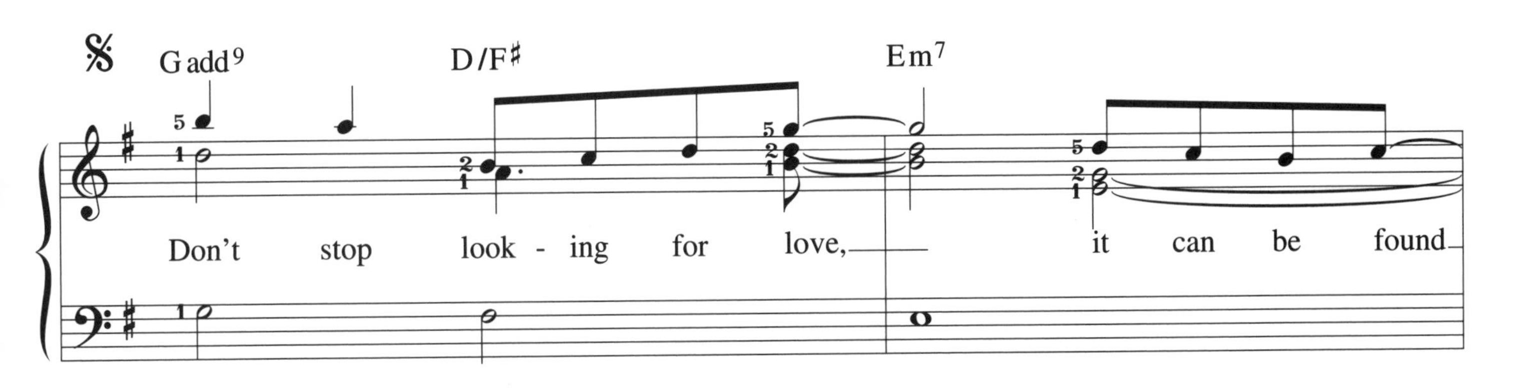
Gadd9
D/F♯
Em7
Don't stop look - ing for love, it can be found

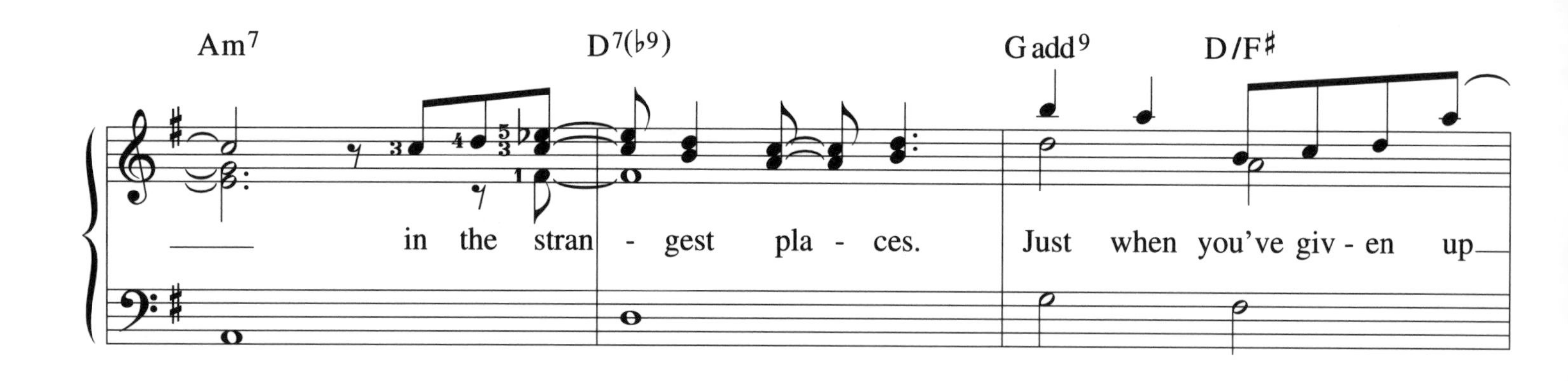
Am7
D7(♭9)
Gadd9
D/F♯
in the stran - gest pla - ces.
Just when you've giv - en up

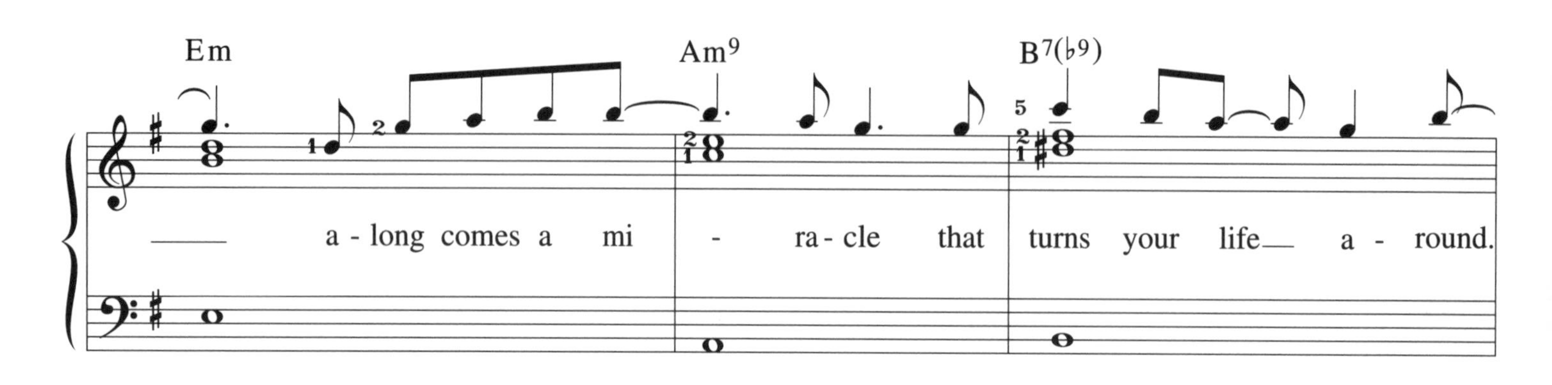
Em
Am9
B7(♭9)
a - long comes a mi - ra - cle that
turns your life a - round.

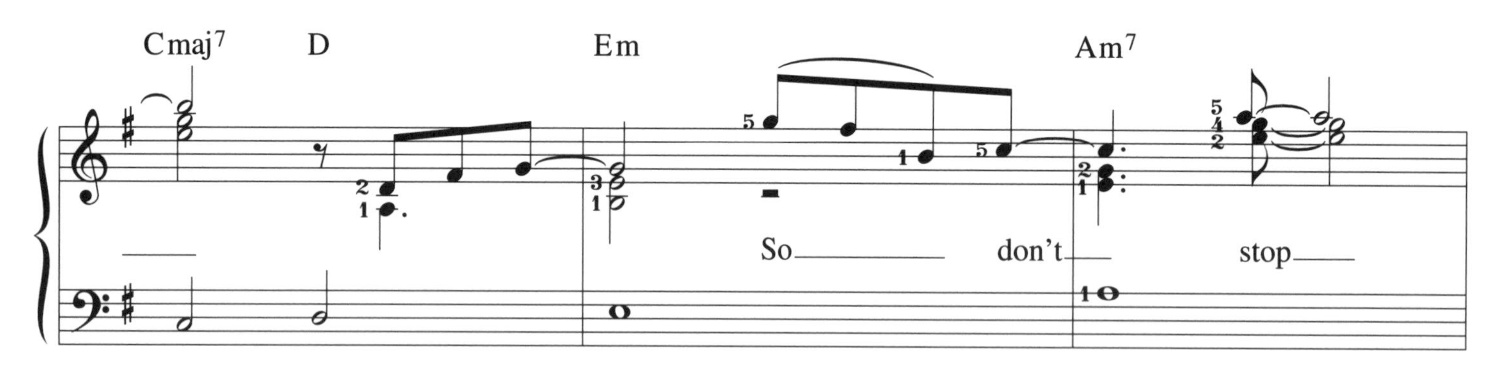
Cmaj7
D
Em
Am7
So don't stop

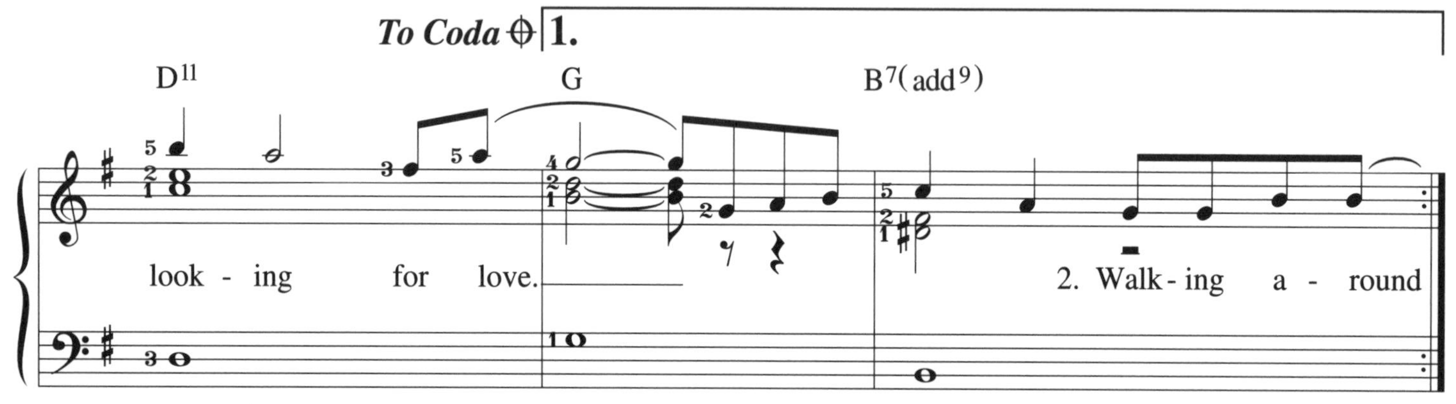
To Coda
1.
D11
G
B7(add9)
look - ing for love.
2. Walk - ing a - round

2.
G
E♭maj7
Dm7
Sud - den - ly my dreams had come and res -

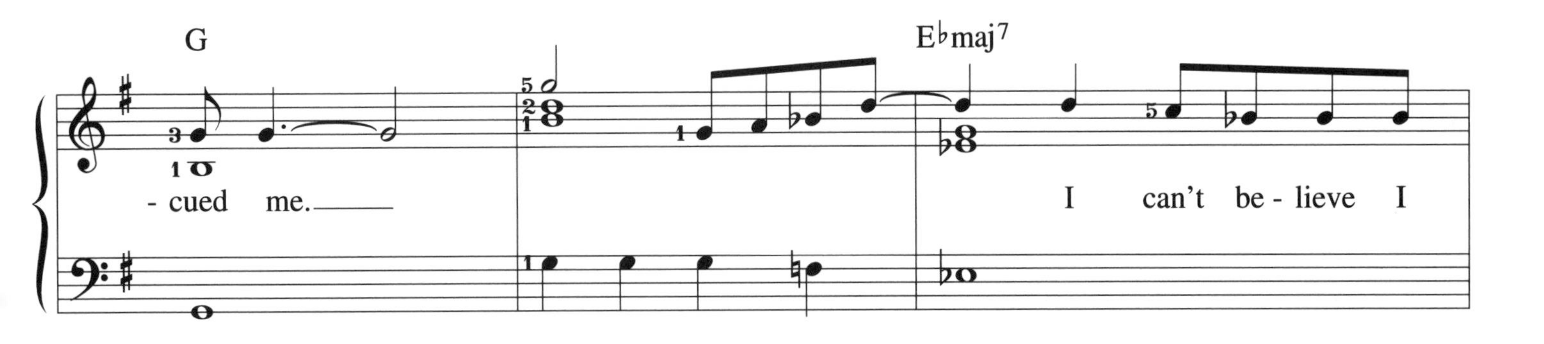

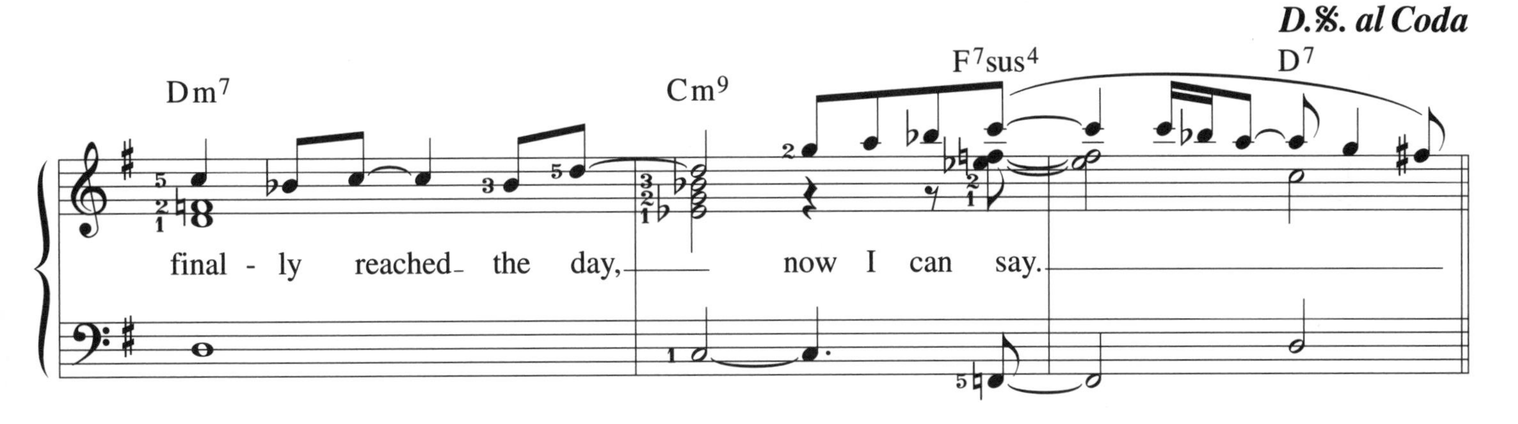

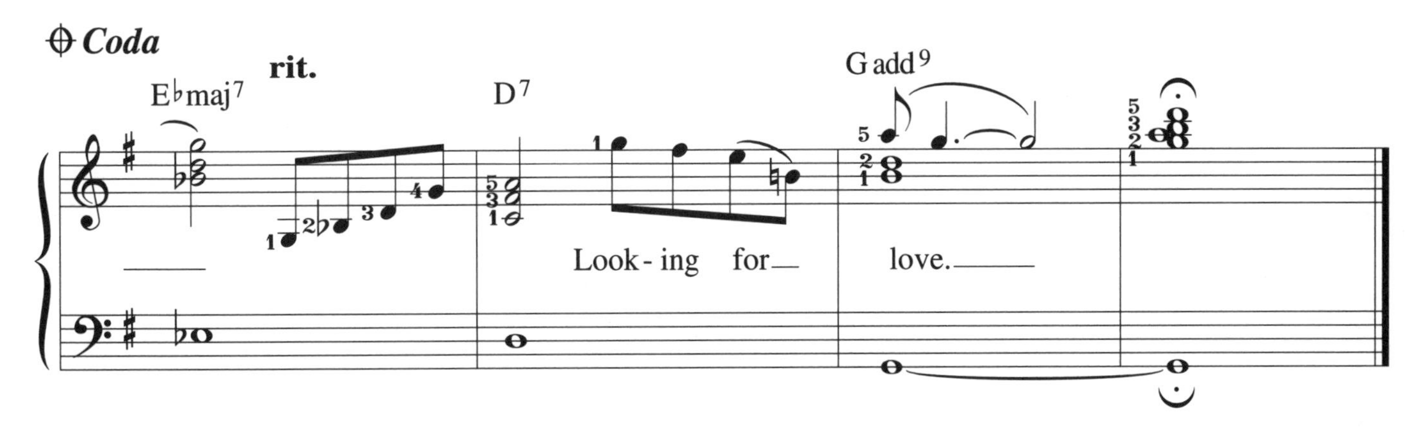

Verse 2:
Walking around with my head hanging down
I felt so all alone.
And your love seemed miles away
I was a heart without a home.
A woman in the rain
You took the clouds away.
Now bright as the sun, our love has begun
And I could hear you say.

games of love

Words & Music by
Martin Brannigan, Stephen Gately & Ray Hedges.

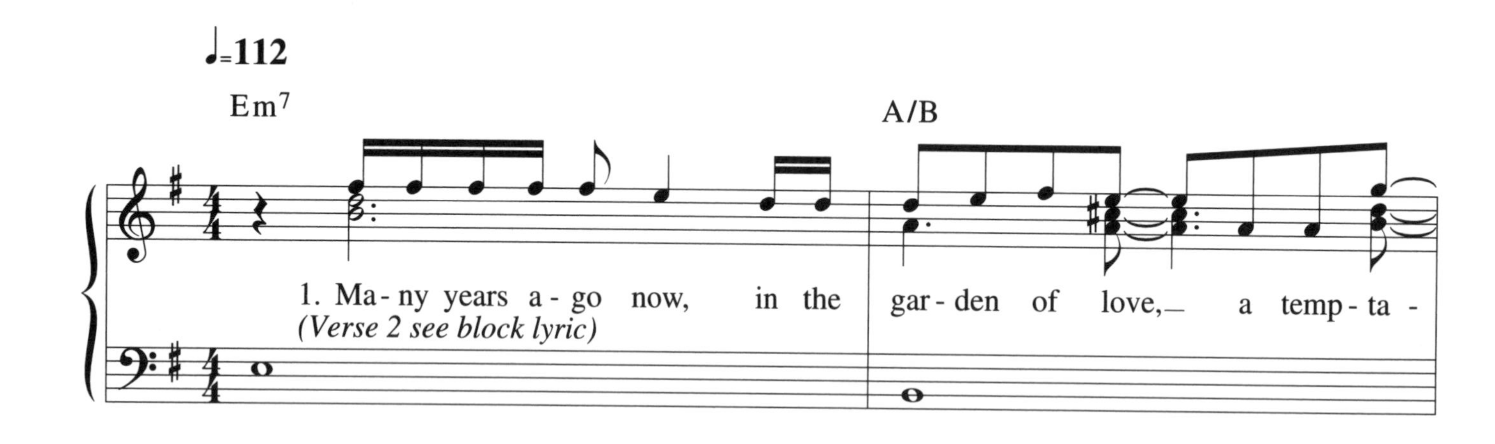

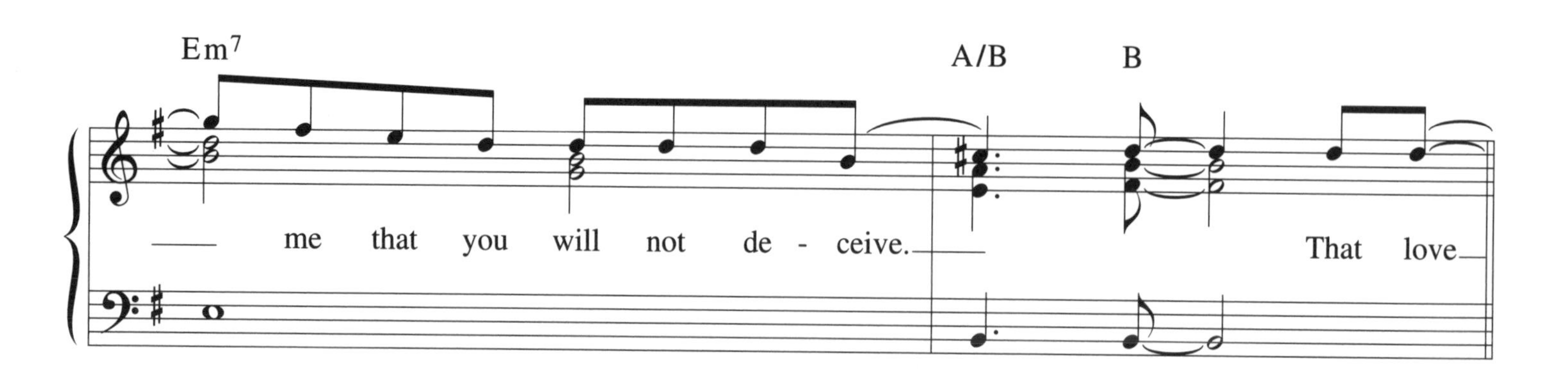

C add9
D
just a cra - zy feel - ing,

C add9
D
deep and hid - den mean - ing, it's true.
And love

C add9
D
takes some un - der - stand - ing, so

B♭6
A
don't you go and break all the rules.
We're talk - in'

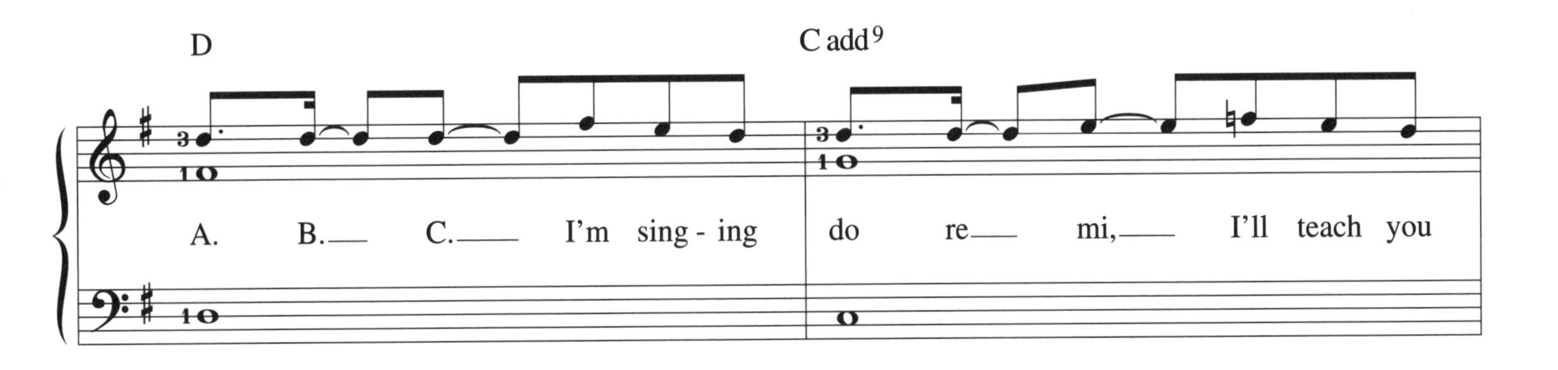
D
C add9
A. B. C. I'm sing - ing
do re mi, I'll teach you

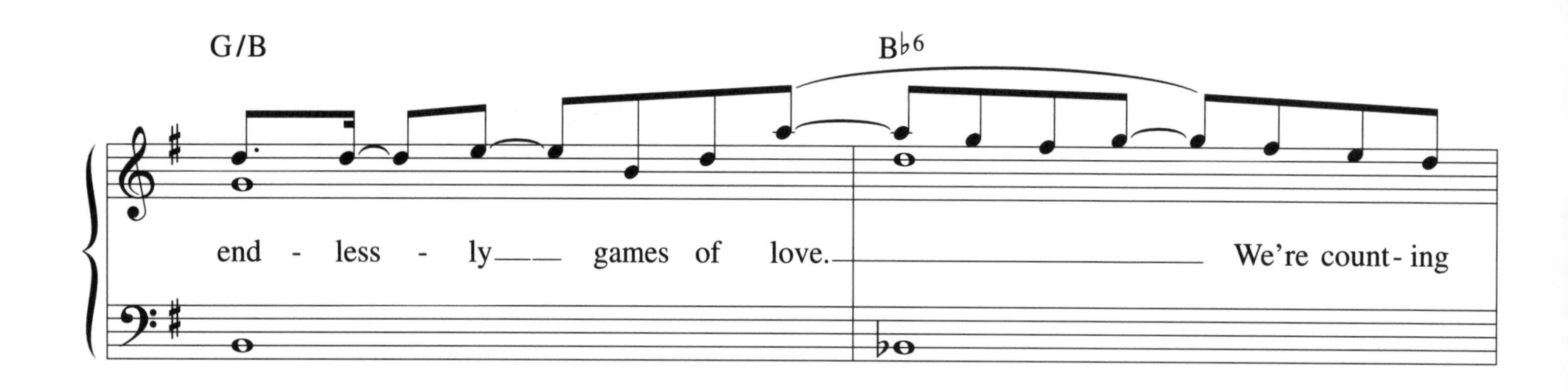
G/B
B♭6
end - less - ly games of love. We're count - ing

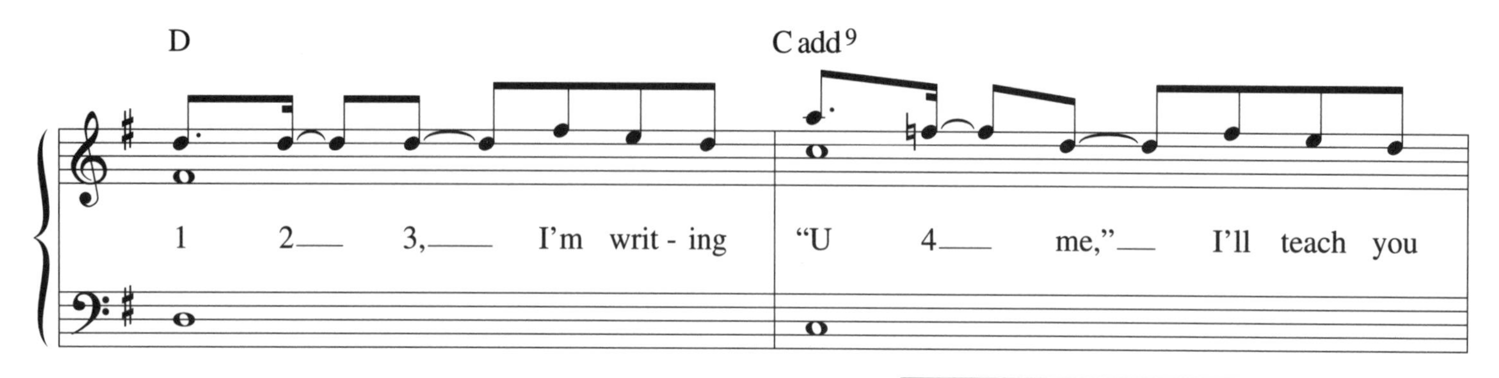
D
C add9
1 2 3, I'm writ - ing "U 4 me," I'll teach you

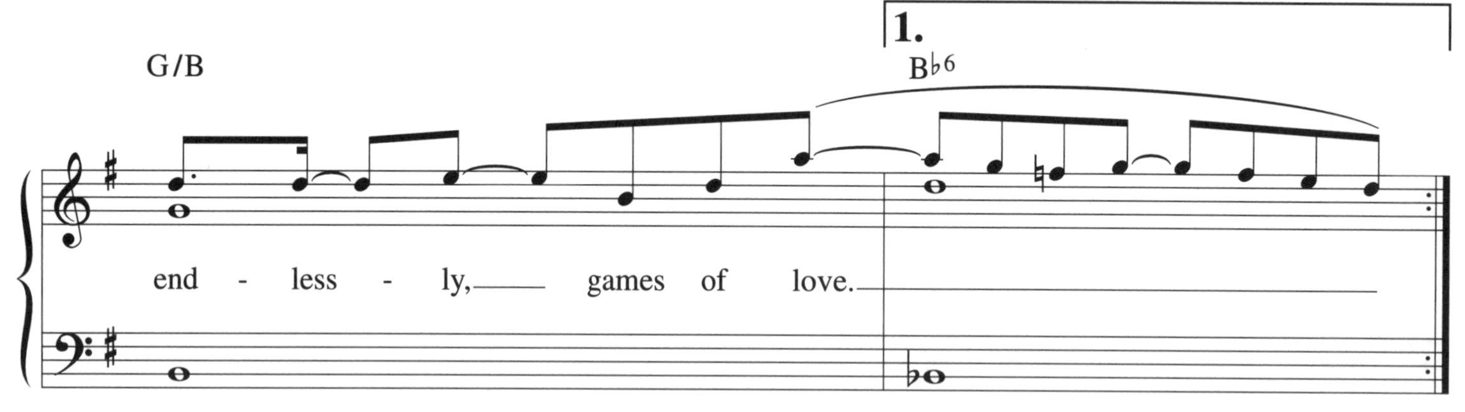
1.
G/B
B♭6
end - less - ly, games of love.

2.
B♭6
D
We're talk - ing A. B. C., I'm sing - ing

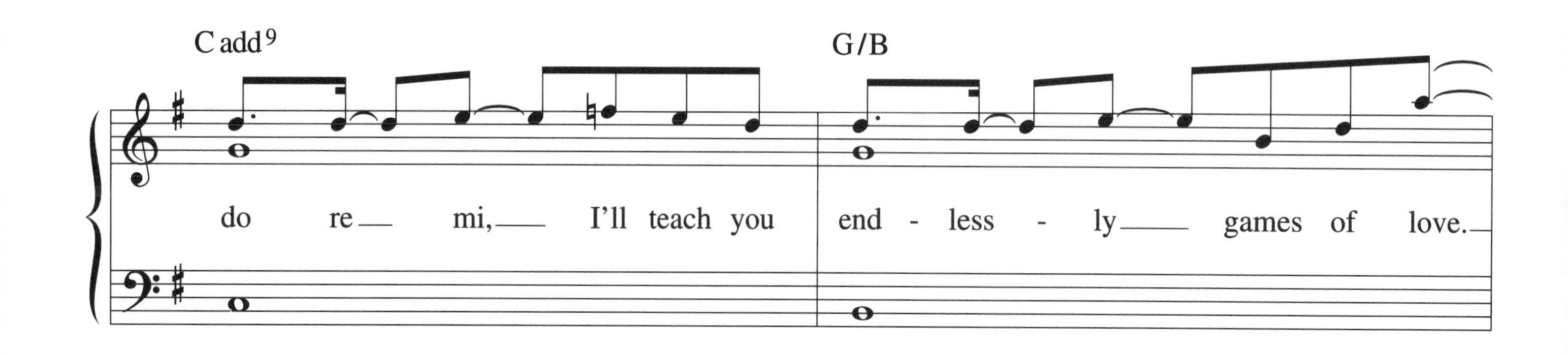
C add9
G/B
do re mi, I'll teach you end - less - ly games of love.

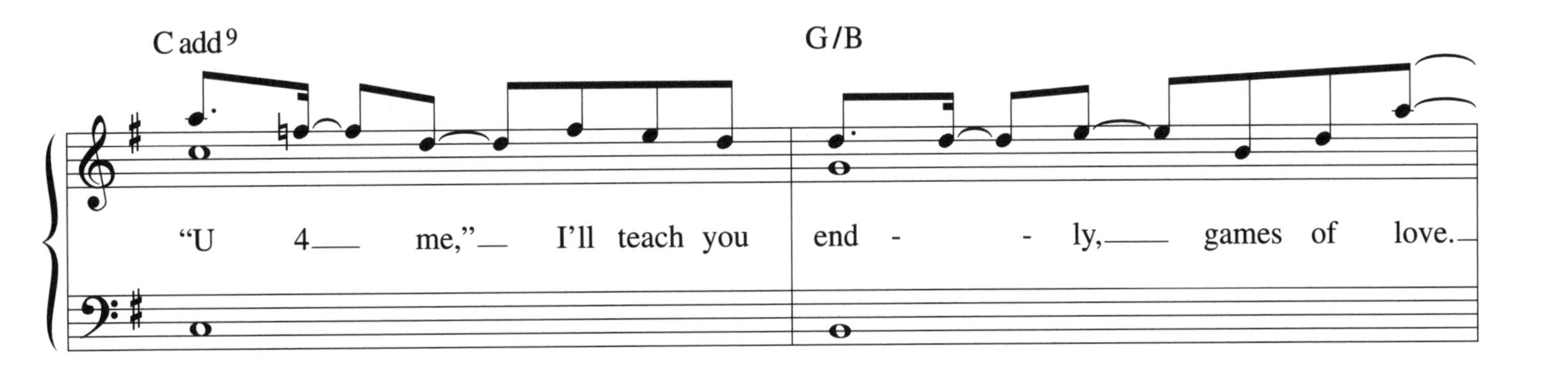

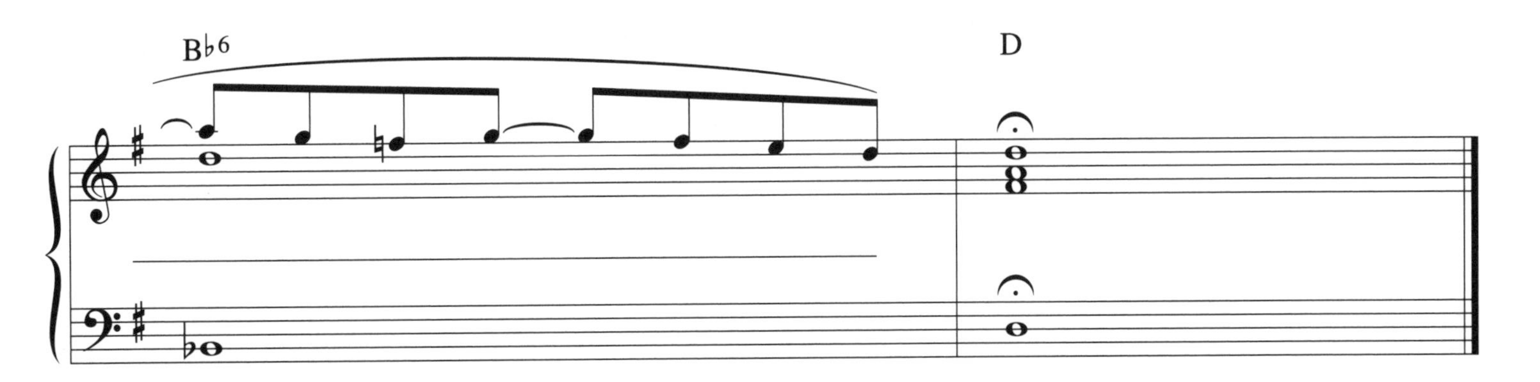

Verse 2:
Listen to me girl 'cause you've known all along
It's a game of love, so don't play it wrong.
I'll be your Romeo and you Juliet
So just read the book and you won't forget.

That love *etc.*

words

Words & Music by
Barry Gibb, Robin Gibb & Maurice Gibb.

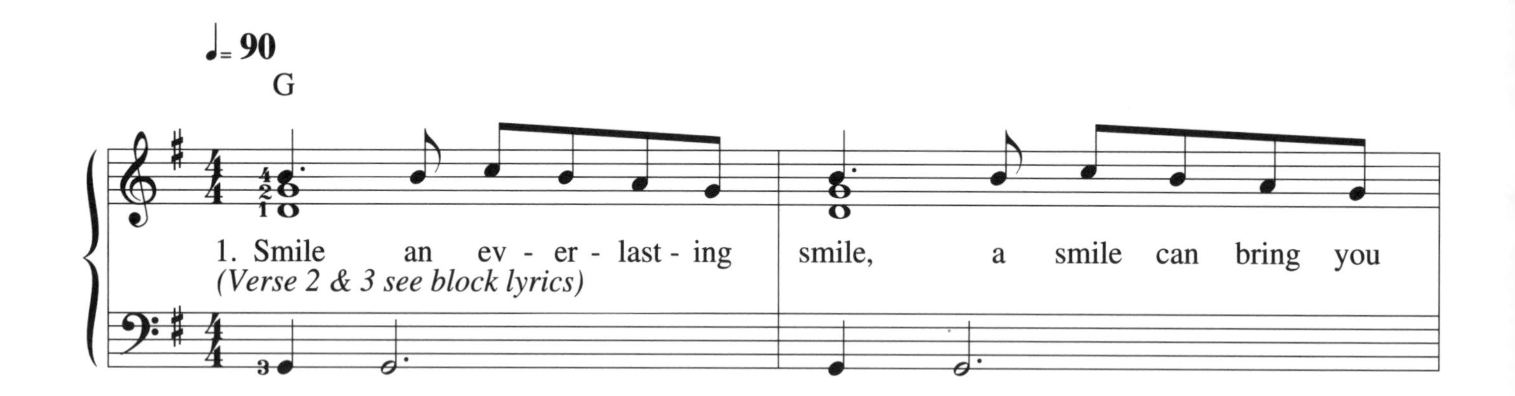

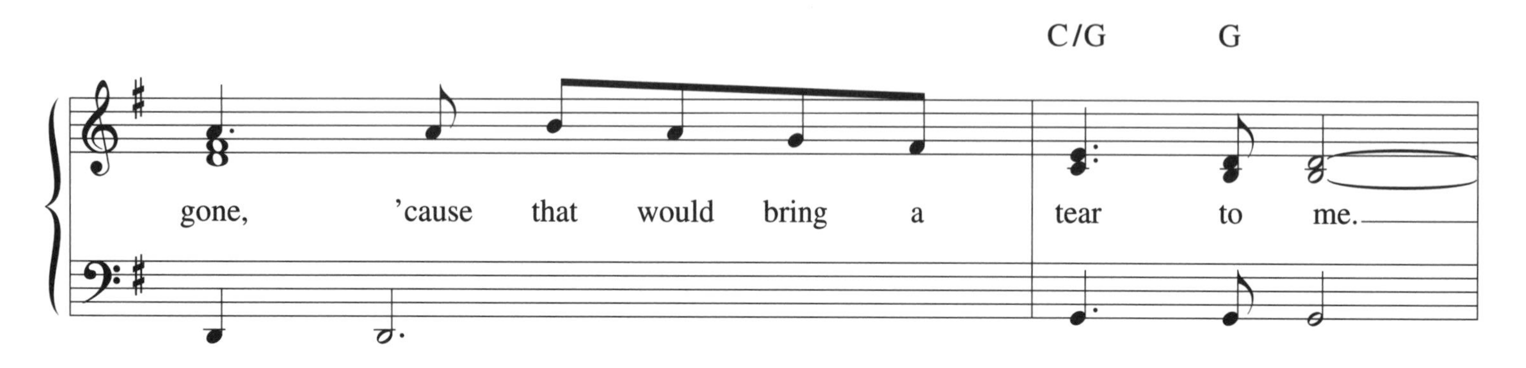

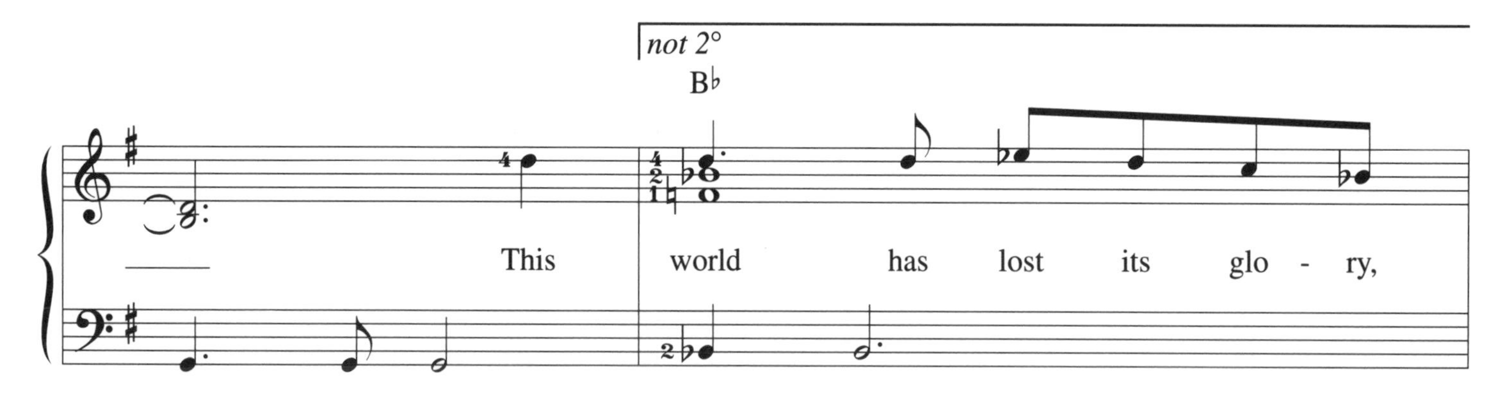

F
let's start a brand new sto - ry
now, my love.
B♭
You
think that I don't ev - en
mean a sin - gle word I
D
say.
It's on - ly
G
words, and words are all I
D
have to take your heart a -
G
- way.
1.
D

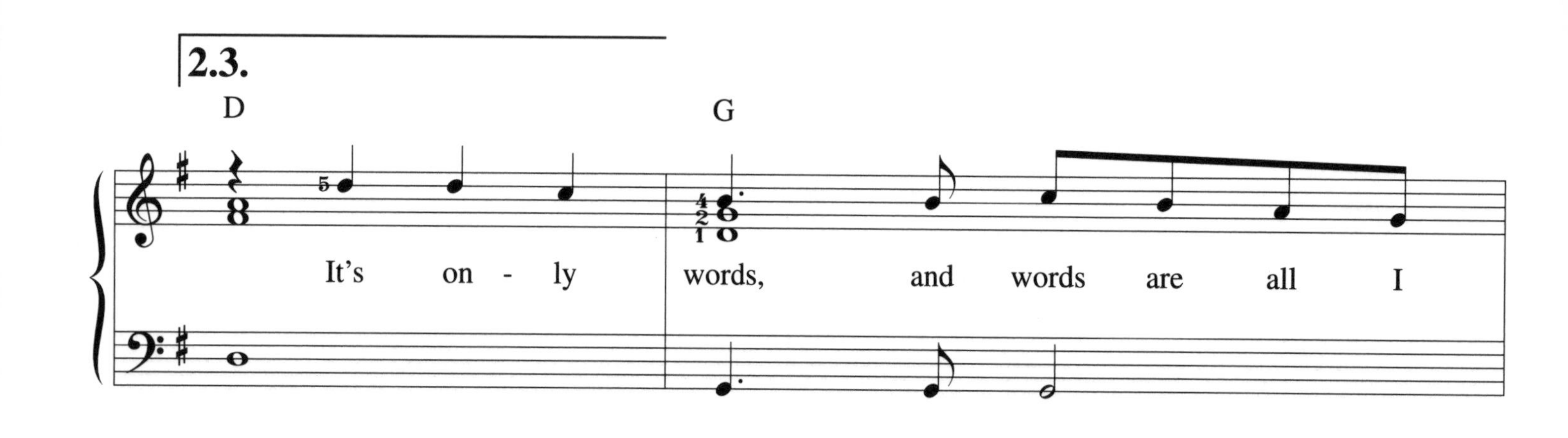

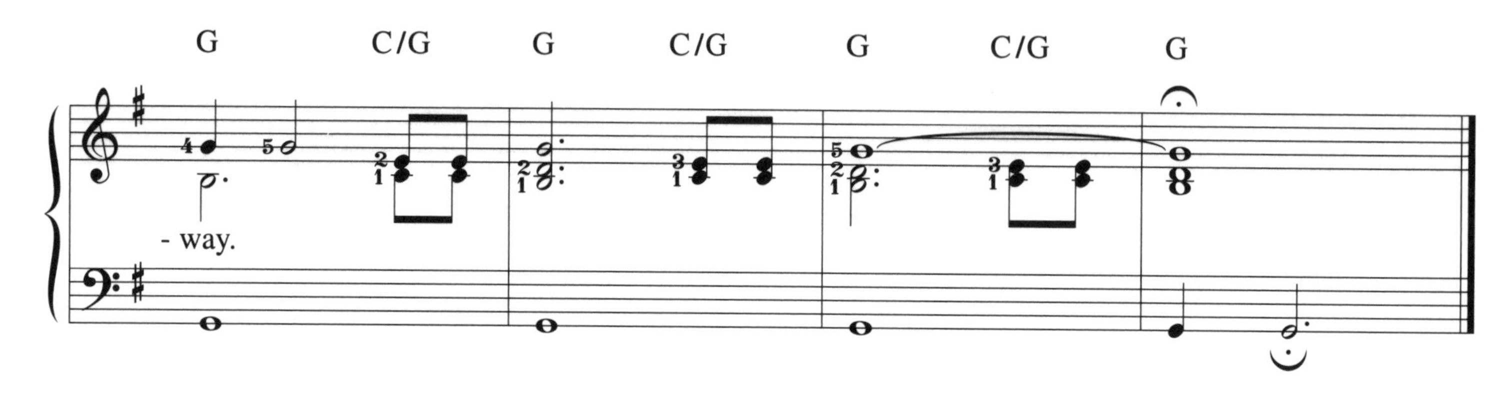

Verse 2:
Talk in everlasting words
And dedicate them all to me
And I will give you all my life
I'm here if you should call to me.

You think that I don't even mean
A single word I say.

Verse 3:
Da da da da… *(8 bars)*

This world has lost its glory
Let's start a brand new story now, my love.

You think that I dont even mean
A single word I say.

baby can i hold you

Words & Music by Tracy Chapman.

1.
2.
Dm9
Fadd9
G
-ly, like sor - ry, like sor - ry.
G11
G
2. For - give me.
G11
C
But you can say ba - by,
Dm7
Fadd9
C
ba - by can I hold you to - night?
Dm7
Fadd9
Am7
Ba - by if I told you the right words, ooh at the right

Verse 2:
Forgive me is all that you can't say
Years gone by and still
Words don't come easily
Like forgive me, forgive me.

all that i need

Words & Music by
Evan Rogers & Carl Sturken.

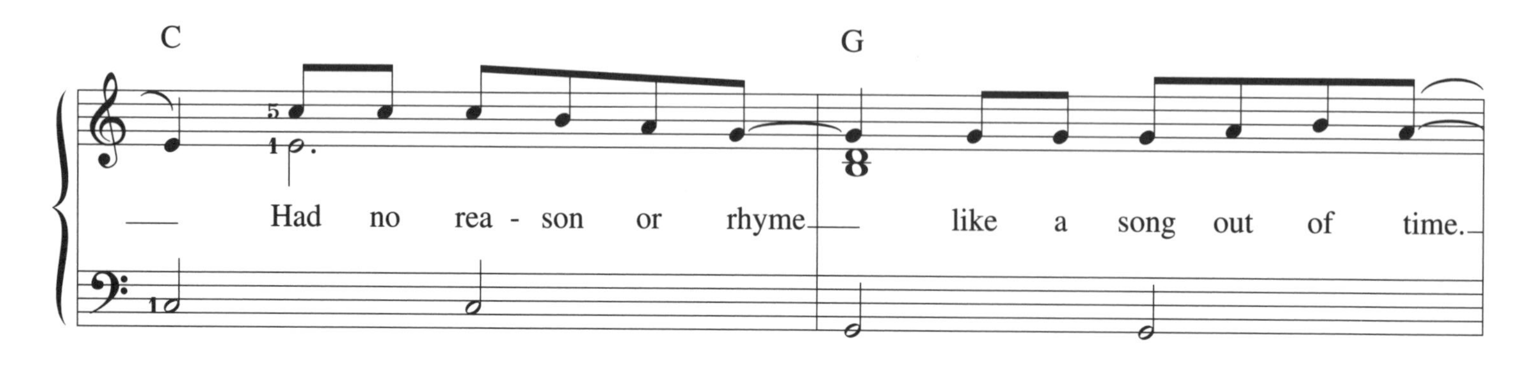

C
G
How could I be such a fool to
Am
Dm7
G11
let go of love and break all of the rules?
C
G
Girl when you walked out that door, left a hole
Am
Dm7
G11
in my heart and now I know for sure;
C
G
You're the air that I breathe girl, you're all that I need,

Am
Dm7
G11
and I wan - na thank you la - dy.
C
G
You're the words that I read, you're the light that I see,
1.
Am
Dm7
G11
and your love is all that I need.
2.
Dm7
G11
that I need.
C
You're the song that I sing,
G
Am
girl you're my ev - 'ry - thing, and I wan - na thank

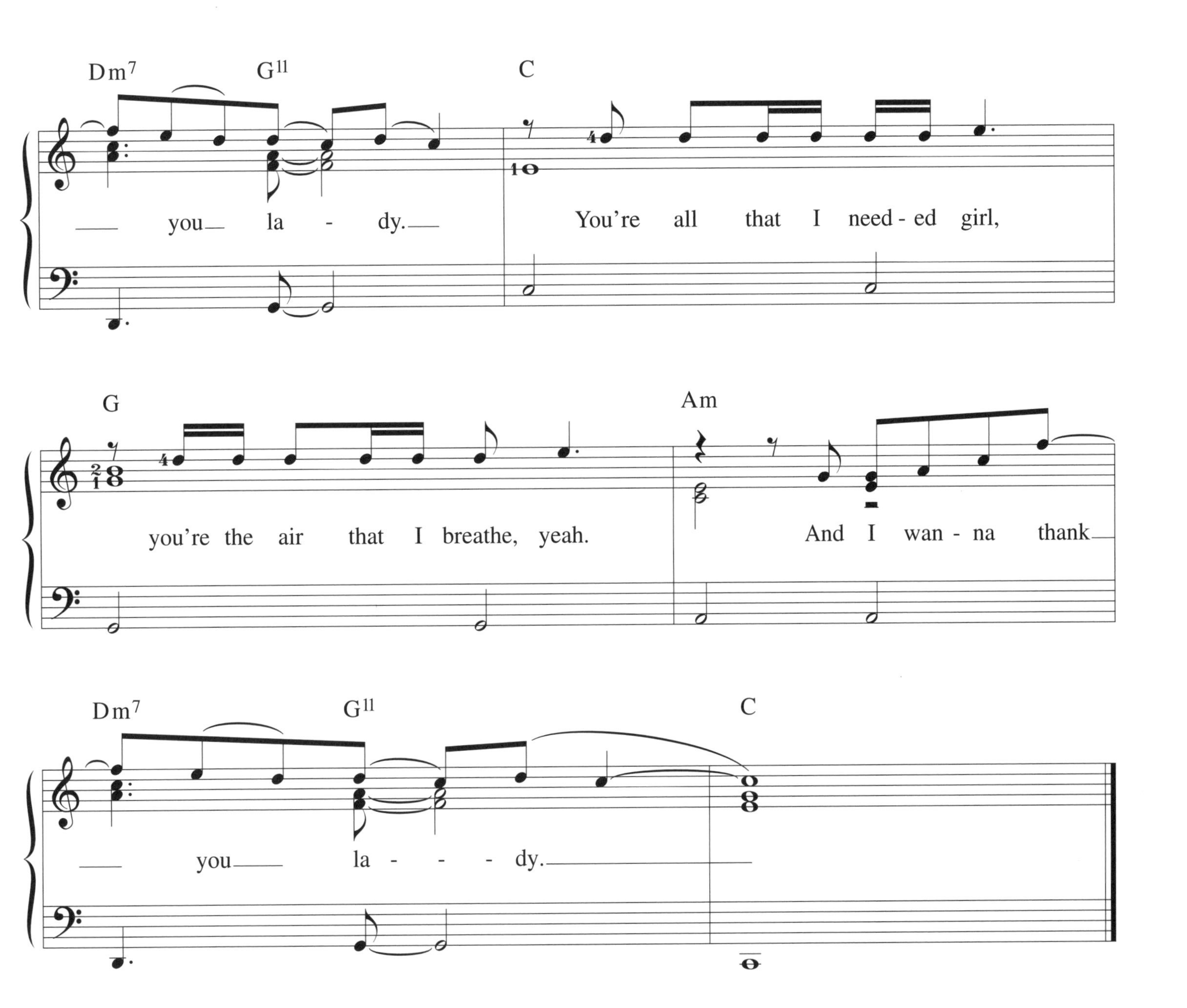

Verse 2:
I was searching in vain, playing your game
Had no-one else but myself left to blame
You came into my world, no diamonds or pearls
Could ever replace what you gave to me, girl
Just like a castle of sand
Girl I almost let love
Slip right out of my hand
And just like a flower needs rain
I will stand by your side
Through the joy and the pain.

You're the air that I breathe *etc.*

picture of you

Words & Music by
Eliot Kennedy, Ronan Keating, Paul Wilson & Andy Watkins.

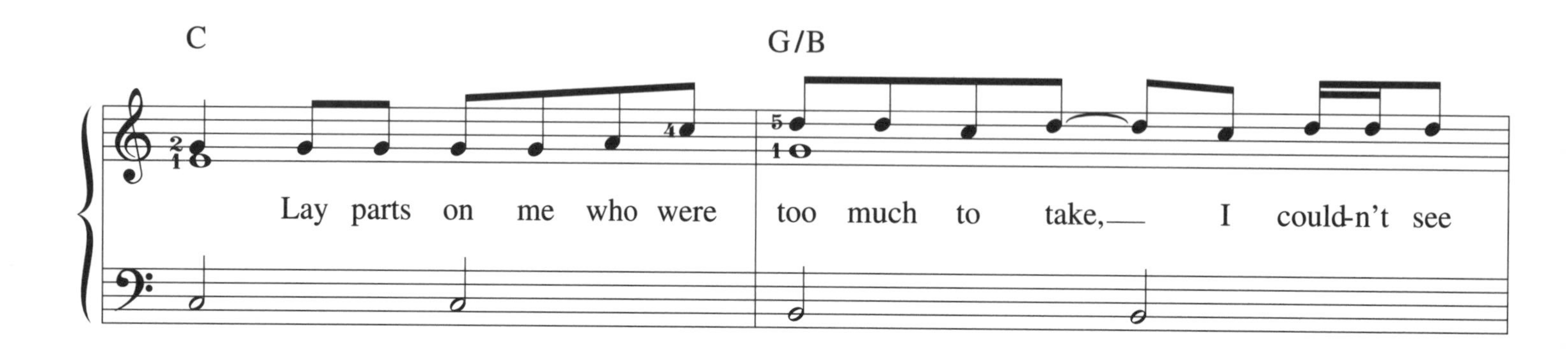

C
G/B
I let you in and you let me down.
(Verse 2 see block lyric)

Gm7
F
G
You messed me up and you turned my life a - round.

C
G/B
Left my feel - ing I had no - where to go, I was a - lone,

Gm7
F
how was I to know that?

Dm11
Am7
G
You were with me there when I need - ed some - bo - dy.

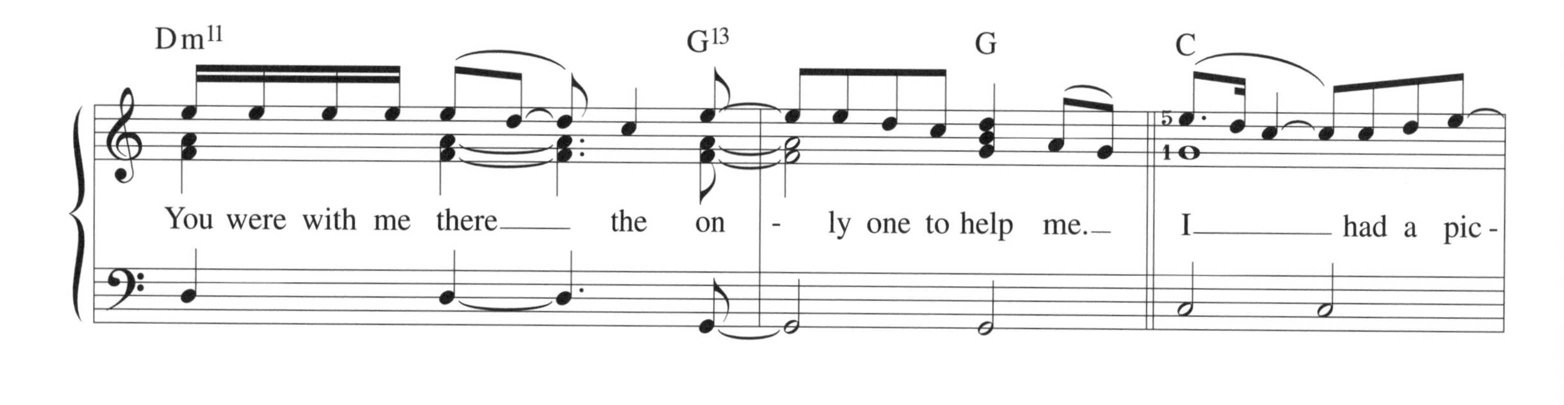

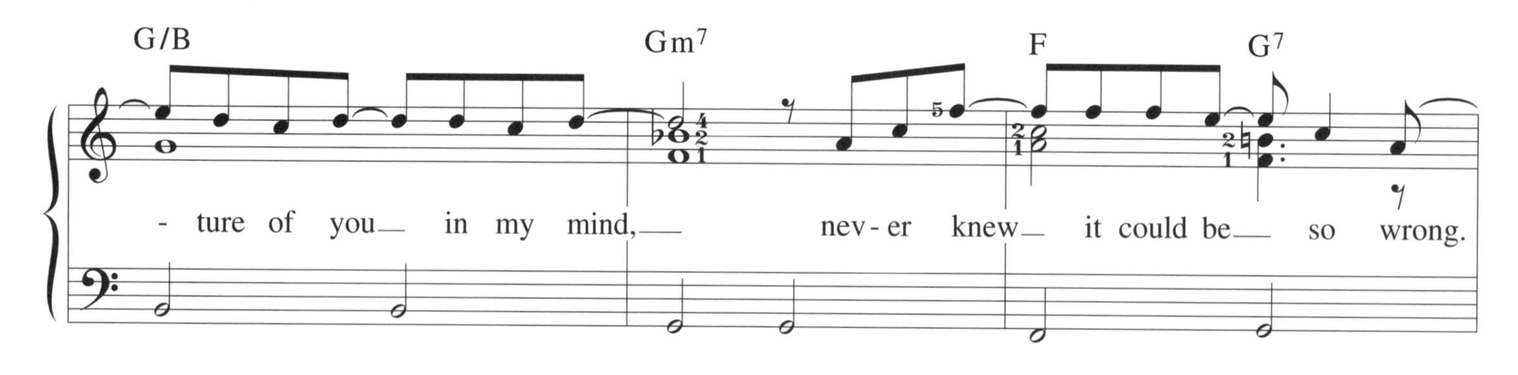

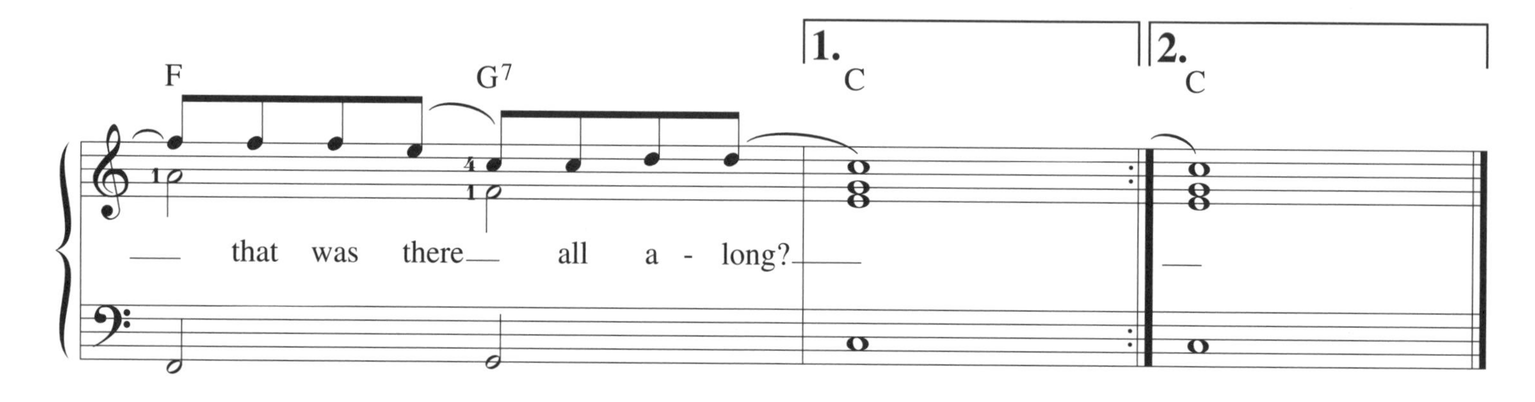

Verse 2:
Do you believe that after all that we've been through
I'd be able to put my trust in you?
Goes to show that you can forgive and forget
Looking back I have no regrets, cos

You were with me there *etc.*

this is where i belong

Words & Music by
Evan Rogers, Carl Sturken & Ronan Keating

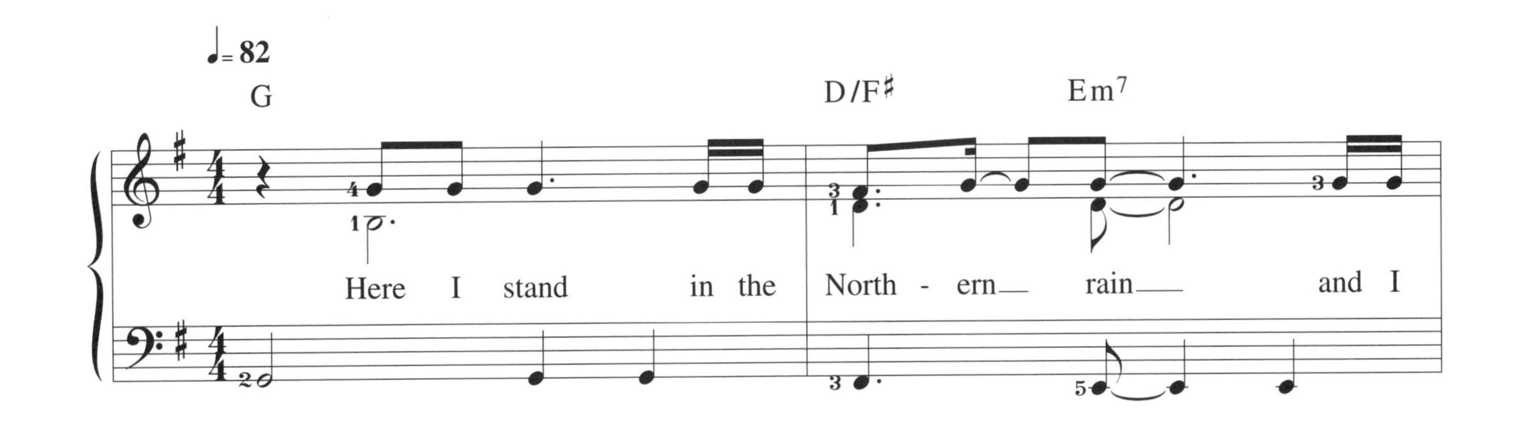

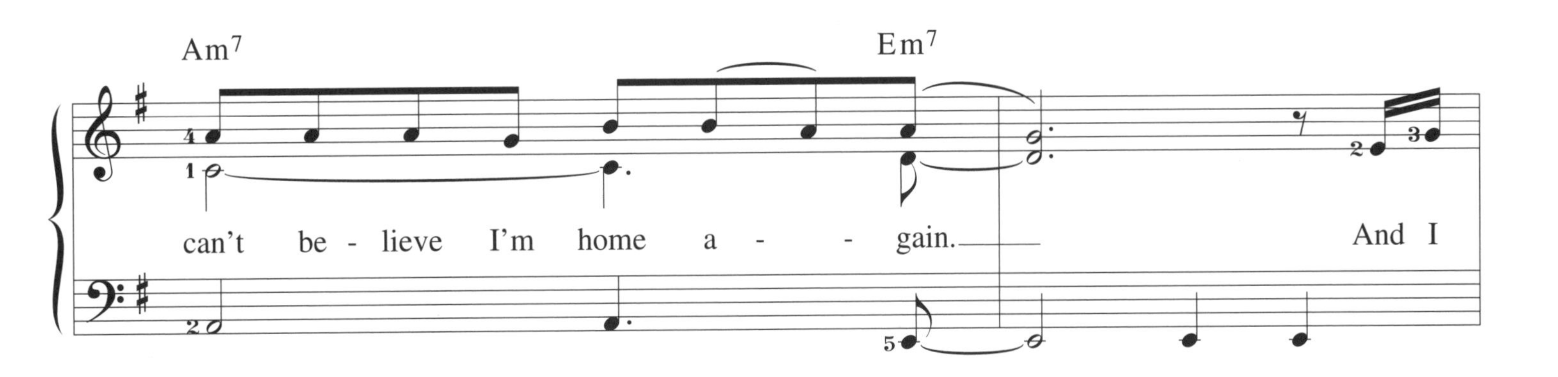

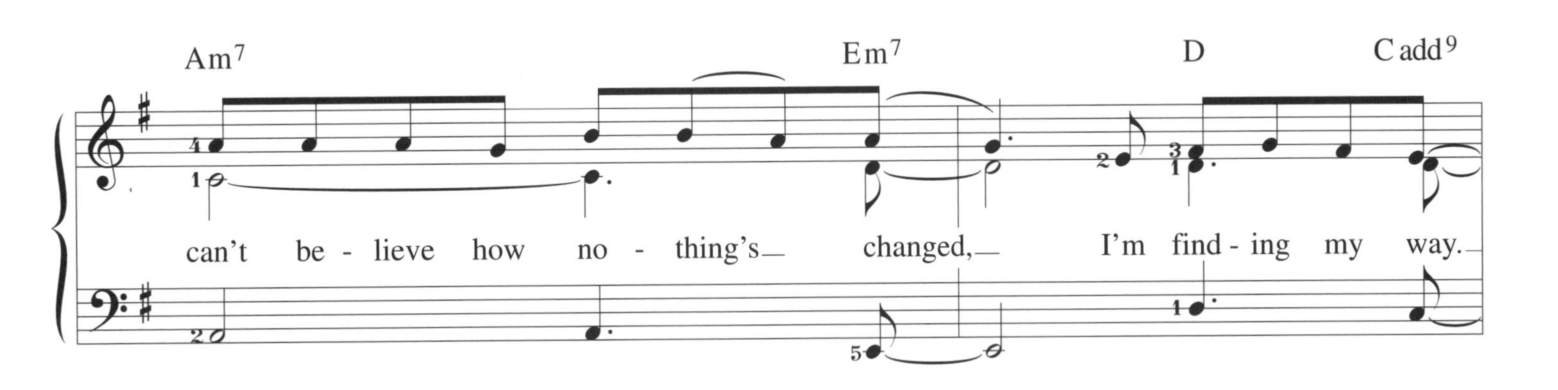

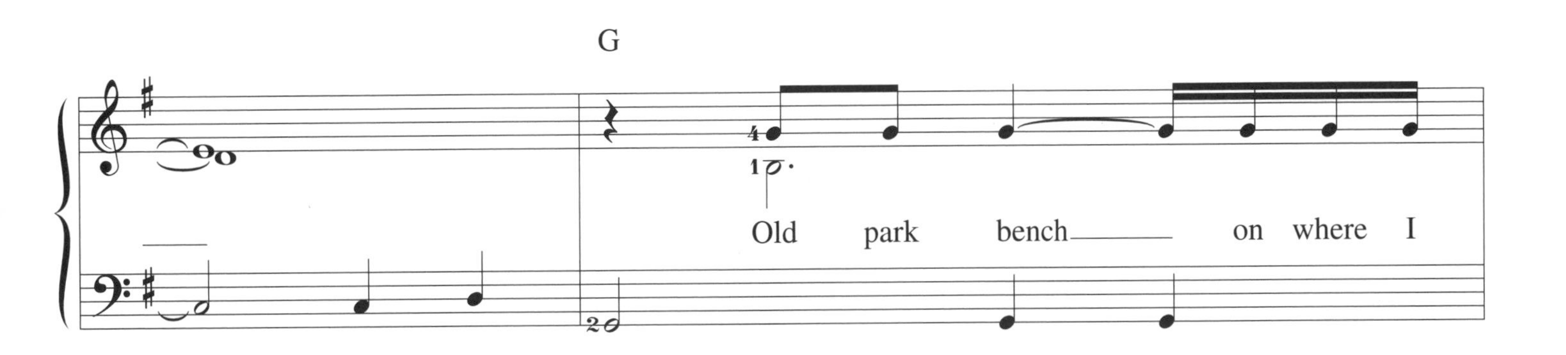

D/F♯
Em7
Am7
Em7
carved my name, but now it does - n't stand a - lone,
Am7
Em7
'cause now the trees have ov - er grown.
D/F♯
G
Am7
Ma - ny a road that I've trav - elled that's
G/B
Cmaj7
A/C♯
D11
led me a - stray, here's where my heart's gon - na stay. This is where I
G
Gmaj9
G
Em7
be - long. This is where I come from.

E11 Em7 C G/B
No need to shed my tears or face my fears a - ny - more.
Am7 D11 G
So I won't walk a - lone.
Gmaj9 G Em7 E11 Em7
Tak - ing things on my own. All of the lands
C G/B B♭maj7
I've roamed, mem-'ries of my home, they keep beat - ing strong,
D11 G
'cause this is where I be - long.

that's how love goes

Words & Music by
Steve Booker & Julian Gallagher

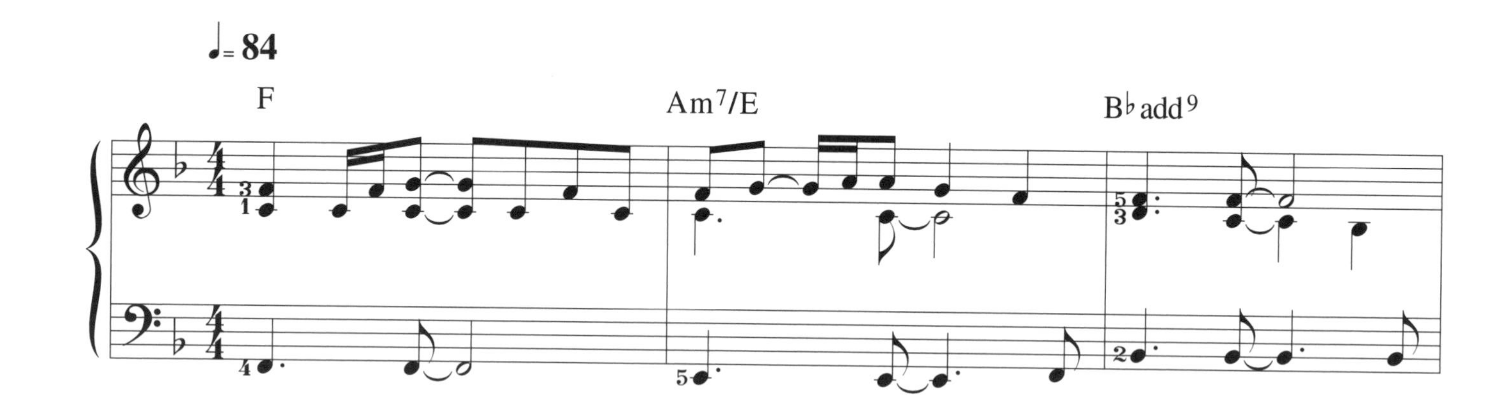

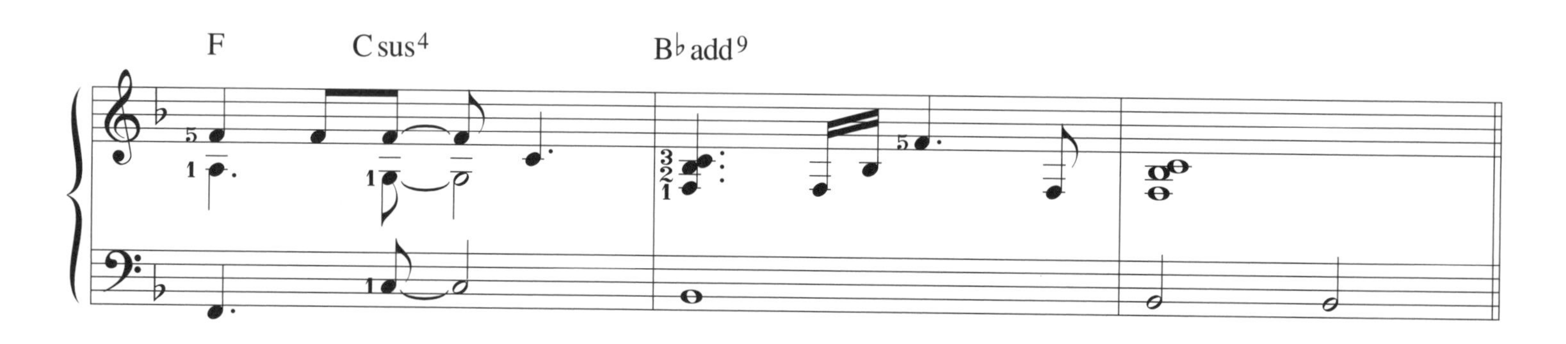

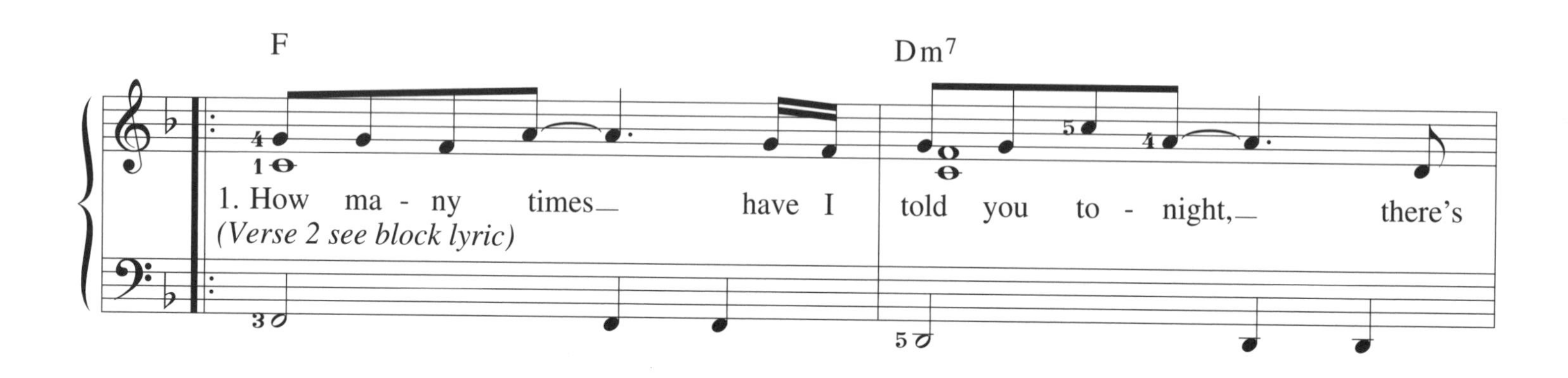

Dm7
don't walk a - way, at the end of the day
B♭add9
F
I won't make you sor - ry if you de - cide to stay.
E♭
Dm7
B♭
Some - times it's hard to hold on,
Gm7
F/A
B♭
C
that's when your heart needs to be strong. That's how
F
Am7/E
B♭add9
love goes, don't ask me why. On - ly love knows what you're

F C F
feel - ing in - side. That's how love goes, one
Am7/E B♭add9
day it's good - bye then it's just one more try.
F C B♭add9
1. 2. B♭11 B♭7
No - bo - dy knows how love goes.
E♭ B♭/D
Some-times it's ea - sy to think you un - der - stand,
Gm7 F/A B♭ Csus4 C
just then you see it slip-ping through your hand. That's how

Verse 2:
The more that I see
The more I believe
That nothing is certain
When you're following your dreams
So all I can do
Is keep holding you
Baby, together
We can make them dreams come true
Sometimes it's hard to hold on
That's when your heart needs to be strong.

That's how love goes *etc.*

These folios contain all the songs from each album in full piano, voice and guitar arrangements. They are complete with lyrics and guitar chord boxes.

where we belong
order no.AM953887

said and done
order no.AM934681

a different beat
order no.AM941644